THE PORTAL OF BEAUTY

THE PORTAL OF BEAUTY

Towards a Theology of Aesthetics

Bruno Forte

Translated by

David Glenday *&* Paul McPartlan

WILLIAM B. EERDMANS PUBLISHING COMPANY

GRAND RAPIDS, MICHIGAN / CAMBRIDGE, U.K.

First published 1999 in Italian as
La porta della bellezza. Per un'estetica teologica

English translation published 2008 by
Wm. B. Eerdmans Publishing Co.
2140 Oak Industrial Drive N.E., Grand Rapids, Michigan 49505 /
P.O. Box 163, Cambridge CB3 9PU U.K.

Printed in the United States of America

14 13 12 11 10 09   7 6 5 4 3

Library of Congress Cataloging-in-Publication Data

Forte, Bruno.
   [Porta della bellezza. English]
   The portal of beauty: towards a theology of aesthetics / Bruno Forte;
   translated by David Glenday & Paul McPartlan.
      p.   cm.
   Includes bibliographical references.
   ISBN 978-0-8028-3280-1 (pbk.: alk. paper)
   1. Aesthetics — Religious aspects — Christianity.
   2. Christianity and the arts.   I. Title.

BR115.A8F6713   2005
230 — dc22

2008036216

www.eerdmans.com

Contents

Introduction

Beauty is an event; beauty happens when the Whole offers itself in the fragment, and when this self-giving transcends infinite distance. But is this really possible? How can the limitless inhabit what is little? How can the everlasting "abbreviate" itself without ceasing to be? And how can immensity become small and still exist?

The answer offered to these questions by an important strand in Western thought is that all this can indeed happen, in one of two ways: either through the *form* of the fragment, the way, that is, that it makes present here and now the harmonious proportions of the Whole — so beauty is "formosus"! — or through beauty's *brightness,* where the splendor of the Whole bursts forth in the fragment, and lays hold of the beholder: this bright loveliness is "speciosus"! In the first case, the Whole finds a home in the fragment inasmuch as the latter lets itself be the particular dwelling-place of the infinite in space and time, by reproducing here and now in an analogical way the harmony which always exists in the Whole; in the second, the Whole breaks forth, as it were, from within what is intimate, opening a window on to the unlimited, and so making the fragment a place where eternity shortens itself in time, and infinity pours itself out into the finite.

Here the Greek soul and Christianity's new way of seeing things meet. Here Christianity makes Athena her own and then betrays her, because — though Christianity, too, longs to contemplate the Whole in the fragment — it proclaims that Beauty happened once and for all in a garden outside Jerusalem's walls. The Cross of Beauty is raised on Calvary hill. In this world, the Word speaks the truth about himself in the ultimate "self-emptying," thanks to that act by which — in no way coerced by the One who is infinitely great — the Son lets himself be contained by the infinitely small. Becoming little in this way is truly divine: "Non coërceri maximo, contineri tamen a minimo, divinum est."[1] At the same time, this ecstasy, this "going out" of God is for us the mightiest conceivable call to live our own going forth from the world, towards the mystery that enthralls us by its saving beauty, present in the "abbreviation" of the Word in the flesh. The Whole dwells in the fragment, the infinite erupts into the finite: the Crucified God is the form and splendor of eternity in time. On the cross, the "Verbum abbreviatum" — the self-emptying of the eternal Word — reveals beauty as "tiny Infinity"!

This, then, is the purpose of this book: while making no claim to say all that might be said, the aim is to consider this singular approach to beauty as it has been developed in various ways down the centuries. There is no intention here of rehearsing either a general theory, or history, of aesthetics as the discipline has been developed in modern times. The purpose is another: to examine the deep, even though not always obvious, contribution of theological thought to the understanding and experience of beauty. Augustine, Aquinas, Kierkegaard, Dostoevsky, Evdokimov, and Balthasar will be called as witnesses, and then, in the light of what they have to say, an attempt will be made to offer a rereading of the beauty that happens in music, cinema, and poetry. Finally, and only *in limine*, attention will be turned to the mysterious bond uniting beauty to the ultimate, silent threshold, where more than ever we find ourselves invited to pass from one side to the other, and at last there opens before us the door of Beauty itself. . . .

---

1. Cf. H. Rahner, "Die Grabschrift des Loyola," in *Stimmen der Zeit* 139 (1946-47): 321-39; G. Fessard, *La dialectique des Exercices spirituals de S. Ignace de Loyola,* I (Paris: Aubier, 1956), pp. 166-77. The phrase, cited in *Imago Primi Saeculi Societatis Iesu* (Antwerp, 1640), p. 280, as "Elogium sepulcrale S. Ignatii," was used by Hölderlin as exergue to the novel *Hyperion* (1794).

Chapter One

DIVINE BEAUTY

Augustine

From One Beauty to the Other

What is the relationship between God and beauty?

Augustine's entire life is a response to this question: it might be said that the whole of his thought was dominated by the twin themes — which he considered intimately intertwined — of God the Trinity and beauty.[1] His interest in the latter was at its most intense in the period preceding the decisive moment of his conversion. Augustine himself recognized this in the deeply moving words of his *Confessions,* where the "you" he invokes is the One he has come to know as beauty itself: "Late have I loved you, O beauty so ancient and so new, late have I loved you!"[2]

Augustine admits that it had been precisely the beauty of creatures that had kept him far from their Creator; he confesses that in the end the Creator and his beauty broke through to him through those very senses by which we perceive beauty in its every appearance:

> Behold, you were within me, but I was outside myself: I sought you here
> and, in my degradation, I threw myself upon the beautiful things that
> you had made. You were with me, but I was not with you. Keeping me
> far from you were those very things which, if they did not exist in you,
> would not exist at all. You called, you cried out, you overcame my deaf-

1. Cf. the well-documented research of J. Tscholl, *Dio e il bello in Sant'Agostino* (Milan: Ares, 1996; German original Leuven, 1967).

2. *Conf.* X, 27, 38: "Sero te amavi, pulchritudo tam antiqua et tam nova, sero te amavi!"

1

ness; you lit up my life like lightning, you shone forth and put my blind-
ness to flight; you breathed forth your sweet smell, I took it in and
yearned for you; you touched me, and I burned with longing for your
peace.[3]

Hearing, sight, smell, taste, and touch: beauty overtakes them all — and
takes them to itself. At first, it is the beauty of created things, but then ultimate Beauty, the source of every other. Augustine's whole story thus becomes a journey from beauty to Beauty, from the penultimate to Ultimate:
only at this journey's end is he able to rediscover the meaning and measure
of the beauty of everything that exists in the light of that which founds every beauty.

One may thus understand how for Augustine to think about God, and
about all things in God, was one with thinking about beauty: when this
theologian speaks of God, he speaks of Beauty, and when he speaks of
what is beautiful in this world, he constantly points to the One who is the
source and goal of all that is beautiful. For Augustine, too, these two
themes of God and beauty are held movingly together by the motif of love:
in fact, beauty has such power over us because it draws us to itself with the
leading strings of love. As Augustine understands it, the call of beauty has
such power over us because it bears within it love's unifying strength. This
is why theology occupies itself with beauty: because theology is both originally and constitutively concerned with the revelation of love, and with
what love means for us. The *Confessions* again:

> In those days . . . I loved a lesser beauty, I was rushing towards the abyss,
> and saying to my friends: Is it not true that we only love what is beauti-
> ful?[4]

It was to remain Augustine's unwavering conviction that we can only
love what is beautiful: "Non possumus amare nisi pulchra."[5] Whether

---

3. *Conf.* X, 27, 38: "Et ecce intus eras et ego foris et ibi te quaerebam et in ista formosa,
quae fecisti, deformis inruebam. Mecum eras, et tecum non eram. Ea me tenebant longe a te,
quae si in te non essent, non essent. Vocasti et clamasti et rupisti surditatem meam,
coruscasti, splenduisti et fugasti caecitatem meam, fragrasti, et duxi spiritum et anhelo tibi,
gustavi et esurio et sitio, tetigisti me, et exarsi in pacem tuam."

4. *Conf.* IV, 13, 20: "Tunc . . . amabam pulchra inferiora et ibam in profundum et
dicebam amicis meis: 'num amamus aliquid nisi pulchrum?'"

5. *De musica* VI, 13, 38.

beauty is enthralling us, or delighting us with its harmony, it is doing nothing other than dancing to the music of love: beauty is to be sought in the "ordo amoris."[6]

At the Wellsprings of Beauty

Where does beauty's power of attraction lie? Why does it attract love? Augustine poses these questions with the greatest of rigor, and certainly also in the light of his own personal experience:

> What is beautiful? And what is beauty? What is it in the things we love that wins us over and attracts us? Since if there were no harmony and beauty in these things, they would not draw us to themselves at all.[7]

Two different answers suggest themselves here: first, that the formal reason for beauty is in the things themselves that appear beautiful to us; second, that the reason why we find something beautiful lies in the subject who finds pleasure in them. In other words: is beauty that which is beautiful, or that which gives pleasure? Is it beauty itself that draws us, or is the attraction itself, and thus the pleasure enjoyed, the origin of our fascination with beauty? "In the first place, I will ask if things are beautiful because they please, or if they please because they are beautiful."[8]

For someone like Augustine, who has worked through to a strong sense of the objective truth which shines forth in the very depths of the world of the subject, there can be no doubt or hesitation in choosing between these two alternatives:

> I will never cease reminding those who have the vision to look into the invisible world of the reason why these things give pleasure, so that they will be able to evaluate human delight itself. . . . They will certainly respond by saying that these things please because they are beautiful.[9]

---

6. Cf. R. Bodei, *Ordo amoris. Conflitti terreni e felicità celeste* (Bologna: Il Mulino, 1991).

7. *Conf.* IV, 13, 20: "Quis est ergo pulchrum? et quid est pulchritudo? quid est quod nos allicit et conciliat rebus, quas amamus? nisi enim esset in eis decus et species, nullo modo ad se moverent."

8. *De vera religione* 32, 59: "Et prius quaeram utrum ideo pulchra sint, quia delectant; an ideo delectent, quia pulchra sunt."

9. *De vera religione* 32, 59: "At ego virum intrinsecus oculatum, et invisibiliter videntem

The beauty of that which is beautiful is not dependent on the taste of the subject, but is inscribed in the things themselves; it has an objective force. And in what does this original structure of beauty consist? Augustine again:

> Then I will ask them why such things are beautiful and, if they hesitate to reply, I will suggest that perhaps they are beautiful because the various parts are similar to each other and, through a kind of intimate relationship, they form a harmonious whole.[10]

Thus the beautiful is that which evinces a deep, harmonious *convenientia* between the different elements of which it is composed, a "con-venire" issuing from the depths:

> Ask yourself what it is that attracts you to physical pleasure, and you will find that it is nothing other than harmony: indeed, while what is disharmonious causes pain, that which is harmonious gives pleasure.[11]

Augustine goes on to develop this idea through an understanding of beauty as the presence of the Whole in the parts of the fragment, where each of these parts is in harmony with the others, and where together they relate to that which is other than themselves:

> I looked carefully and saw that, in corporal beings, one thing is the whole and thus the beautiful, while another is that which is harmonious because well adapted to something other than itself, like a part of the body to the whole or a shoe to the foot.[12]

For Augustine, beauty happens thus: the whole appears by way of the proper mutual interrelationship between the parts which compose the

---

non desinam commonere cur ista placeant, et iudex esse audeat ipsius delectationis humanae. . . . Hic mihi sine dubitatione respondebitur, ideo delectare quia pulchra sunt."

10. *De vera religione* 32, 59: "Quaeram ergo deinceps, quare sint pulchra; et si titubabitur, subiciam, utrum ideo quia similes sibi partes sunt, et aliqua copulatione ad unam covenientiam rediguntur."

11. *De vera religione*, 39, 72: "Quaere in corporis voluptate quid teneat, nihil aliud invemnies quam convenientiam: nam si resistentia pariant dolorem, convenientia pariunt voluptatem."

12. *Conf.* IV, 13, 20: "Et animadvertebam et videbam in ipsis corporibus aliud esse quasi totum et ideo pulchrum, aliud autem, quod ideo deceret, quoniam apte acconmodaretur alicui, sicut pars corporis ad universum suum aut calciamentum ad pedem."

fragment, and so by way of a form which reproduces this harmonious composition of the elements in unity, and in which the essence (or *species)* of the thing in question becomes evident:

> It is no accident that when we praise something we use both the terms *speciosissimum* (that which has the essence to the highest degree) and *formosissimum* (that which has the form to the highest degree).[13]

Beauty is thus understood as intrinsic to the object, and so to be distinguished from a mere functionality or adaptability by which the object is capable of corresponding well with that which is other than itself: "Pulchrum, quod per se ipsum, aptum autem, quod ad aliquid adconmodatum deceret, definiebam."[14] The kind of unmerited enjoyment evoked by Beauty is thus well expressed by the term *frui*, a delight that is its own justification, while functionality is best expressed by the term *uti:*

> To use [*uti*] something is to place it at the disposal of the will, while to enjoy it [*frui*] is to use it with that delight which is no longer merely hope, but possession. So those who enjoy something may also be said to use it, because they dispose of it at will and it thus gives them delight. Instead, those who simply use something do not always enjoy it, as is the case when the thing placed at the disposal of their will is not desired for itself, but to some other end.[15]

Augustine thus introduces the distinction "between rationality directed to purpose and rationality directed to value. From certain points of view, the term *uti* substantially translates the logic of the former, while *frui* better expresses the latter."[16]

Now the object of supreme joy, love, and perfect enjoyment (*frui*), and thus the unity that is the source and goal of every unity of the parts and of every beauty, is God alone. God

13. *De vera religione* 18, 35: "Neque enim frustra tam speciosissimum, quam etiam formosissimum in laude ponitur."

14. *De vera religione* IV, 15, 24.

15. *De Trinitate* X, 11, 17: "Uti enim est assumere aliquid in facultatem voluntatis; frui est autem uti cum gaudio, non adhuc spei, sed iam rei. Proinde omnis qui fruitur, utitur; assumit enim aliquid in facultatem voluntatis, cum fine delectationis. Non autem omnis qui utitur fruitur, si id quod in facultatem voluntatis assumit, non propter illud ipsum, sed propter aliud appetivit."

16. Bodei, *Ordo amoris,* p. 152.

is the beginning to which we return, the form we follow, the grace by which we are reconciled: God alone, by whose hand we were created, in whose likeness we were formed in unity, and by whose peace we hold fast to unity . . . the only one by whose creative work we live, by whose regeneration we live in wisdom, and through whom, loving whom and enjoying whom [*quem diligentes et quo fruentes*], we live in blessedness: the only God from whom, through whom and in whom are all things.[17]

The unity which makes its appearance in the fragment, the wholeness which manifests itself there in the harmony between the parts, is thus only a reflection of that wholeness and unity which are found in God: it is God who is that eternal beauty of which we will never tire, "pulchritudo tam antiqua et tam nova"! Augustine knows this well, and he orders everything, both in his thought and in his life, towards this last horizon:

> His entire work and all his ideas about the *ordo amoris,* about the human trinity or the *civitas Dei,* aim to render rationally plausible the logic of *frui* which cannot be proven, calling on faith in the invisible to lend support to the proofs provided by the visible.[18]

True and eternal beauty reaches our inner selves by way of what may be called the spiritual "senses," which Augustine describes in an analogy with the bodily senses:

> What am I loving when I love you? Not bodily beauty nor the graceful-ness of age; nor light's brightness, so dear to these eyes of mine; not the sweet melodies of song, nor the fragrance of flowers, of perfumes, of aromas; not manna, nor honey; not the body so dear to the embraces of the flesh: no, these are not the things I love when I love my God. And yet in a certain sense I do love light and sound, smell and food and embrace, when I love my God, the light, sound, smell, food, and embrace of my inner being. There, a light shines for my soul untrammeled by space; there, I hear a sound that does not disappear into time; there, I smell a

17. *De vera religione* 55, 113: "Principium ad quod recurrimus, et formam quam sequimur, et gratiam qua reconciliamur: unum quo auctore conditi sumus, et similitudinem eius per quam ad unitatem formamur, et pacem qua unitati adhaeremus . . . unum Deum quo creatore vivimus, per quem reformati sapienter vivimus, quem diligentes et quo fruentes beate vivimus: unum Deum ex quo omnia, per quem omnia, in quo omnia."

18. Bodei, *Ordo amoris*, p. 152.

perfume that the wind does not carry off; there, I savor things that no gluttony makes sickly; there, I experience an embrace never to be broken by surfeit. All this I love when I love my God. So then I asked the earth, "What is all this?" and it replied: "It is not me." And all the things on earth gave me the same answer. I quizzed the sea and its depths, the living things that move there, and they replied: "We are not your God, seek higher." . . . And then I said to all those things seated before the door of my senses, "If it is not you, tell me something about my God, speak to me of him." And with a mighty voice all cried: "He is our creator." I looked at the creatures, and asked; their beauty was their answer.[19]

Creaturely beauty thus points us back to the Creator, by way though of our inner selves, when we perceive this beauty and recognize its ultimate source, its supreme reference:

So learn to recognize what constitutes the most perfect harmony: do not go out of yourself, but enter into yourself; truth lives in your inner self and, if you find that your nature is changeable, transcend even yourself. But remember, when you go beyond yourself, that you are going beyond your rational soul: tend, thus, to the place where the very light of reason burns.[20]

---

19. *Conf.* X, 6, 8: "Quid autem amo, cum te amo? Non speciem corporis nec decus temporis, non candorem lucis ecce istis amicum oculis, non dulces melodias cantilenarum omnimodarum, non florum et unguentorum et aromatum suaviolentiam, non manna et mella, non membra acceptabilia carnis amplexibus: non haec amo, cum amo deum meum. Et tamen amo quandam lucem et quandam vocem et quendam odorem et quendam cibum et quendam amplexum, cum amo Deum meum, lucem, vocem, odorem, cibum, amplexum interioris hominis mei, ubi fulget animae meae, quod non capit locus, et ubi sonat, quod non rapit tempus, et ubi olet, quod non spargit flatus, et ubi sapit, quod non minuit edacitas, et ubi haeret, quod non divellit satietas. Hoc est quod amo, cum Deum meum amo. Et quid est hoc? Interrogavi terram, et dixit: 'Non sum'; et quaecumque in eadem sunt, idem confessa sunt. Interrogavi mare et abyssos et reptilia animarum vivarum, et responderunt: 'Non sumus Deus tuus: quaere super nos.' . . . Et dixi omnibus his, quae circumstant fores carnis meae: 'Dicite mihi de Deo meo, quod vos non estis, dicite mihi de illo aliquid.' Et exclamaverunt voce magna: 'Ipse fecit nos.' Interrogatio mea intentio mea et responsio eorum species eorum."

20. *De vera religione* 39, 72: "Recognosce igitur quae sit summa convenientia. Noli foras ire, in teipsum redi; in interiore homine habitat veritas; et si tuam naturam mutabilem inveneris, trascende et te ipsum. Sed memento cum te transcendis, ratiocinantem animam te transcendere. Illuc ergo tende, unde ipsum lumen rationis accenditur."

Augustine's understanding of beauty thus in no way excludes the mediation of the subject. This, though, is not made absolute, but rather becomes the path along which the various forms taken by penultimate beauty are able to point us towards the harmony of supreme beauty; it is the subject which perceives the presence of the Whole in the fragment, where the harmony and unity of the parts point to that Whole which is ultimate and original unity, from which and in which exists all that exists.

Victorious Beauty

Beauty is composed of these constitutive elements:

> *aequalitas (parilitas), similitudo; congruentia, convenientia, concordia, pax, ordo; totum, simul omnia, unitas; distinctio, varietas, gradatio; mensura, dimensio, numerositas; mensura — species — ordo. . . .*[21]

This kind of terminology certainly echoes the classical lexicon, but here it is employed with a new emphasis, because all these relationships are not understood statically in themselves, but are referred to their ultimate source, to which they all point as their origin and homeland, that is, God. Nor do these things point to God in a kind of vague continuity, but rather in a way which takes account of the abyss, bridged only by creation, of the freely effected and offered work of divine Beauty. Thus it is that only the inner self is able to move from one beauty to the Other, from the penultimate to the ultimate, because only the eyes of a reason which transcends even itself are able to glimpse that vision which surpasses every vision, thus fulfilling our original human ability to look upon God.

> The true proportion and similarity, as well as the true and original unity, cannot be seen by the eyes of the body or by any other sense, but only by an act of understanding.[22]

It is this spiritual journey which makes it possible for Augustine to perceive the beauty present even in what at first sight may appear

---

21. Tscholl, *Dio e il bello in Sant'Agostino*, p. 40.

22. *De vera religione* 30, 55: "Porro ipsa vera aequalitas ac similitudo, atque ipsa vera et prima unitas, non oculis carneis, neque ullo tali sensu, sed mente intellecta conspicitur."

beauty's opposite, such as pain or deformity: from transcendent to Transcendent, from form to Form, he glimpses a yet higher and deeper order even in the opposite of beauty, such that all things work together towards the harmony planned by the supreme artificer, and such that everything is beautiful when seen in him as its ultimate source. God is praised even by darkness![23]

The fact that such an inner journey is necessary in order to perceive true beauty indicates, however, the ambiguity that always lies in wait when we experience creaturely beauty, for this can seduce and distract us from the beauty of the Creator, to whom instead it ought by its very nature to refer. This is due, though, not to the ugliness of the creatures, but rather to the deformed vision of those who let themselves be blinded by sin and darkness, so as to become no longer able to discern the beautiful harmony that points us to the divine plan:

> Since corruption does not belong to the soul by nature, but against its nature, and since it does not consist in anything other than sin and in the punishment of sin, one may clearly understand that no nature or substance or essence is bad. . . . It is thus not the beauty of the whole of creation that is to be held responsible for the damnation of sinners, for the testing of the just, or for the perfection of the blessed.[24]

Here too, though, a plan of beauty makes itself manifest, precisely in the justice and mercy that God uses towards those who have let themselves be taken in by the sweet delight of lesser goods:

> It is the beauty of justice, in harmony with the grace of kindness, that, after we have being led astray by the sweetness of lesser goods, we are taught by the bitterness of punishment.[25]

---

23. Cf. *De natura boni* 8 and 16.

24. *De vera religione* 23, 44: "Quoniam igitur vitium animae non natura eius, sed contra naturam eius est, nihilque aliud est quam peccatum et poena peccati; unde intelligitur nullam naturam, vel . . . nullam substantiam sive essentiam malum esse. . . . Et est pulchritudo universae creaturae per haec tria inculpabilis; damnationem peccatorum, exercitationem iustorum, perfectionem beatorum."

25. *De vera religione* 15, 29: "Et est iustitiae pulchritudo cum benignitate gratia concordans, ut quoniam bonorum inferiorum dulcedine decepti sumus, amaritudine poenarum erudiamur."

Thus ultimate beauty is victorious over all its seeming opposites: just as everything that exists only exists because of love, so everything is beautiful, because supreme Beauty touches everything it loves, even when weak eyes or a heart wounded by evil are unable to perceive this Beauty's mysterious and fruitful presence. . . .

So it is that for Augustine the whole universe is like a network of interconnected realities which refer us back, by way of their harmonious interrelationship, from the unity and beauty of individual creatures to the unity and beauty of the Creator, from whom all beauty comes. A two-way movement traverses this network: beauty comes down to us, and we go up to supreme beauty. The first movement is revelation: eternal Beauty becomes flesh and makes itself perceptible to the senses of our outward selves, so that our inner selves might be touched and captured by the grace which frees and saves us. For Augustine, the Word is the pure enactment of Beauty, because it is the Truth of perfect unity with the first Beginning:

> We understand that there is something so similar to the Only and the Unique, the Beginning from which issues the unity of all that is in some way one, that it is able to achieve this Beginning in itself and to identify us with it: this is the Truth, the Word which was in the beginning, God the Word with God.[26]

The incarnate Word is the way by which we are able to gain access to ultimate Beauty:

> Our life came down among us; he took our death upon himself, he slew it by the superabundance of his life, and with a voice of thunder he called out to us so that we might return and find him in that secret place whence he came to us in the virgin's womb. . . . He withdrew from our sight that we might enter into ourselves, and find him there. He went away, and, behold, he is here.[27]

---

26. *De vera religione* 36, 66: "Datur intellegi esse aliquid, quod illius unius solius, a quo Principio unum est quidquid aliquo modo unum est, ita simile sit ut hoc omnino impleat ac sit idipsum; et haec est Veritas et Verbum in Principio, et Verbum Deus apud Deum."

27. *Conf.* IV, 12, 18: "Et descendit huc ipsa vita nostra et tulit mortem nostram et occidit eam de abundantia vitae suae et tonuit clamans, ut redeamus hinc ad eum in illud secretum, unde processit ad nos in ipsum primum virginalem uterum. . . . Et discessit ab oculis, ut redeamus ad cor et inveniamus eum et ecce hic est. Noluit nobiscum diu esse et non reliquit nos."

Jesus the Word leads us to the source of beauty, though, because he draws us with the leading-strings of love: here we perceive the second movement that runs through beauty, the upward movement of a love which responds, evoked by the love which came to us as grace and freedom. All things are drawn towards, and yearn for, the supreme unity of God, one and three, created as they are by the Father through the Word to return to the Father through him:

> So in him and with him we also venerate Truth itself, in no way dissimilar from him, who is the form of all the things which were made by the One and tend towards the One. Spiritual souls thus clearly perceive that all things were made according to this form, which alone fulfils the desires of all things.[28]

So we can say that everything that exists comes from the Trinity and is drawn towards the Trinity: "In the Trinity is to be found the supreme source of all things, and perfect beauty, and complete joy."[29] It is this being-drawn to the supremely Beautiful, this love, which breathes through the whole movement of creation's return to the Creator: the beauty of ultimate Love evokes the love of beauty, which little by little draws our inner selves to travel the path that leads to perfect joy in God, who is all in all. The path of Beauty is thus shown to be the way leading to God the Trinity, and hence the way to salvation and truth: in beauty everything is made one, and all things find their ultimate meaning.

So the deepest reality of everything that exists is beauty, through which — coming from God and pointing back to him as eternal and supreme beauty — everything is beautiful and capable of being beautiful. To the purified eye of our inner selves, touched by the beauty of God, is revealed that which is closed and sealed to those imprisoned by penultimate beauties: Beauty — ultimate and true Beauty, which draws with the strings of no passing love — is the salvation of the world! Unity, order, and love are thus equivalent terms to express what underpins everything that exists

28. *De vera religione* 55, 113: "Quare ipsam quoque Veritatem nulla ex parte dissimilem in ipso, et cum ipso veneremur, quae forma est omnium, quae ab uno facta sunt, et ad unum nituntur. Unde apparet spiritalibus animis, per hanc formam esse facta omnia, quae sola implet quod appetunt omnia."

29. *De Trinitate* VI, 10, 12: "In illa enim Trinitate summa origo est rerum omnium et perfectissima pulchritudo et beatissima delectatio."

in the care of creative and welcoming Beauty. God is this Beauty, original and final: so it is that this-worldly beauty, echoing its divine origin and pointing towards its fulfillment in the homeland, is the way that leads to him if, following this way, we do not halt at what is penultimate, but let ourselves be attracted towards supreme delight.

From form to form, from splendor to splendor, everything comes from God the Trinity who is love, and everything moves towards the love of the Trinity. The Greeks' wise understanding of beauty is thus taken up and surpassed: yes, the harmony of the forms is certainly the key, but the movement of transcendence which runs through this — the bridge thrown over the abyss by God's creative act — leads us far beyond a beauty which is ultimately this-worldly, towards the land — savored now as anticipation and pledge — of eternal beauty. The question, though, remains: is it really true that in the end this beauty can justify the disorder and evil that devastate the world? Has the death of Beauty at the hour of abandonment on the Cross already been completely taken up and forever resolved in the victory of Easter? Or does the paradox of the Crucified One challenge us to seek out other paths towards Beauty? Here, Augustine himself seems to urge us to go beyond Augustine. . . .

Chapter Two

THE WORD OF BEAUTY

Thomas Aquinas

The Other Beauty

The history of Christian theology witnesses to the fact that, beyond and alongside the Augustinian tradition, the relationship between theology and beauty has been understood in an alternative and equally great way. One expression of this second approach is offered in the words of Richard of St. Victor, which echo an approach which runs through the entire reflection on the faith: the spontaneity of what Richard has to say, for all that he may be considered a "minor" voice, witnesses to how widespread this approach has been. In his *De unitate Dei et pluraliter creaturarum,* he takes up afresh the ancient problem of the One and the many, so characteristic of Greek and, more generally, of Western thought; there is an awareness here that at stake in the whole reflection on ἐν καὶ πάν is the very meaning of becoming, the solidity or absolutely contingent nature of everything that mortals are and do on this earth. Richard surprises by how he sets about resolving the tension between these two worlds: for him, the riotous life of the many and the quiet tranquility of the One meet in beauty. Beauty alone is that place without place where all things are led back to the One, where the *reductio ad Unum* comes to pass for all things. God, the unspeakable, the Other, dwells here: in this abyss where everything finds unity and peace, in this last place which is our destiny because it is our mysterious, silent origin.

    Richard affirms:

Deus a quo pulchrum est quidquid pulchrum est, et sine quo nihil pulchrum esse potest — God from whom all that is beautiful takes its beauty, and without whom nothing can be beautiful.[1]

God is not beauty: this tradition does not define beauty, nor does it circumscribe it; it seeks instead its deepest source, "a quo pulchrum est." It guards beauty in silence, not wishing in any way to violate it: this is why it issues in the mystical tradition. This approach to beauty stands in the tradition that joins monastic theology to the great flowering of mysticism in the later part of the Middle Ages and the early modern period. Deeply felt here is how the Ultimate draws us beyond all that is penultimate: to travel beauty's path is to be led to walk unfamiliar ways, to know exile, to savor solitude. Beauty can only be encountered in the many this-worldly realities by following a movement upwards, away from self and into unknown distances.

In fact Richard is but one witness to the power of an idea that comes from afar and runs through the whole of Christian thought. Suffice it to recall the words of that mysterious but unanimously respected and beloved teacher, Pseudo-Dionysus the Areopagite:

This divine yearning brings ecstasy so that the lover belongs not to self but to the beloved. . . . This is why the great Paul, swept along by his yearning for God and seized of its ecstatic power, had this inspired word to say: "It is no longer I who live, but Christ who lives in me." Paul was truly a lover and, as he says, he was beside himself for God, possessing not his own life but the life of the One for whom he yearned, as exceptionally beloved. . . . In short, both yearning and the object of that yearning belong to the Beautiful and the Good. They preexist in it, and because of it they exist and come to be.[2]

Beauty is "ecstatic": it can only be attained by those disposed to lose themselves, ready to be led beyond themselves towards the other in a love which impels them beyond every thing, beyond being, beyond even the divine and the good, when these are understood outside of a total exodus from self and from every possession of self.[3]

1. *De unitate Dei et pluralitate creaturarum* 1, 6; Latin text ed. and trans. E. Martineau (Saint-Lambert des Bois: Édit. Établi, 1987), p. 74.

2. *De divinis nominibus* 4, 13: PG 3, 712. English translation: *Pseudo-Dionysius: The Complete Works*, trans. Colm Luibhéid (New York: Paulist, 1987), p. 82.

3. Cf. B. Forte, *L'universo dionisiano nel Prologo della "Mistica Teologia,"* in *Medioevo* 4

It is not difficult to see how this approach, more concerned with a vertical, "ecstatic" dynamism than with Augustine's ordered and harmonious relationships, might lead to an understanding of beauty as simply seductive and with no real transcendence, a kind of supreme continuation of eroticism, excluding crisis and the need for μετάνοια. And yet it is no less possible to see how this same vertical, "ecstatic" movement, now viewed as beginning from above, may lead well beyond the analogy of forms between this-worldly and divine beauty, again characteristic of the Greeks and Augustine, to an explicitly Christological theological aesthetic: this, in fact, is the path traveled by Thomas Aquinas. In the creative power of his genius, he took up and developed this second line of thought, without neglecting the gains made by Augustine. Here, the key employed to understand beauty is not only the idea of the abyss that draws us into itself, or unspeakable otherness, or mysterious and tranquil transcendence that calls out to us. Here beauty is perceived as making itself present and perceptible in a fragment: here it hides *sub contraria specie* in the face of the One before whom we cover our faces, but whose countenance is yet the most beautiful among the sons of men (cf. Isa. 53:3 and Ps. 44:3).

The way into beauty posited here has its starting point in contemplation of the Son of God both revealed and hidden in the flesh. Even if this understanding of beauty still employs the categories of "transgression" and "excess," it nevertheless reverses the approach which focuses on an "ecstatic beauty" centered on the passionate power of divine love which carries the beholder off toward that which is above and outside of all else that is. This alternative approach leads into the tragic reality of that self-emptying which was accomplished in the paschal mystery: here death exists in the world, as in God, in order that there may be fullness of life, and here ecstasy is not in the first place the ascent of human beings to God, but much more the descent of God towards all that is different from himself, even though willed and created by him. Thus it is that Thomas points to the Word as the specific and characteristic place where beauty is revealed. In Part I of his *Summa Theologica* he writes,

> *Pulchritudo* habet similitudinem cum propriis Filii — Beauty is concerned with what is proper to the Son.[4]

(1978): 1-57; now also in Forte, *Sui sentieri dell'Uno. Saggi di storia della teologia* (Milan: Edizioni Paoline, 1992), pp. 11-64.

4. *Summa Theologica* I, q. 39, a. 8c. On the aesthetics of St. Thomas cf. U. Eco, *Il pro-*

Son as Beauty

As a further explanation of this statement he adds that three things must be present for beauty to exist: *integritas, proportio,* and *claritas:*

> Nam ad pulchritudinem tria requiruntur. Primo quidem, integritas sive perfectio. . . . Et debita proportio sive consonantia. Et iterum claritas —
> Thus for beauty to exist three things are required: integrity or perfection . . . due proportion or harmony. And luminosity.

Thomas perceives how these three realities are present in the Son, beginning obviously from how he revealed himself as sent by the Father, as the incarnate and crucified Word.

Beauty is first related to *integritas,* which is the *perfectio* through which the thing in question attains completeness:

> Perfectio est forma totius, quae ex integritate partium consurgit —
> Beauty is the form of the whole, which issues from the integrity of the parts.[5]

In beauty it is the whole that renders itself present and perceptible:

> The integrity of a work is only perceived by those who know how to see the whole *in the very act* of breathing a soul into the various parts, building them, as it were, into itself, reclaiming them for itself, and disposing them in an harmonious order.[6]

In this way, the whole of the divine mystery dwells in the Word, because it is the nature common to the Three that is present and at work in the person of the Son, as it is in each of the other two:

> Quantum igitur ad *primum,* similitudinem habet cum proprio Filii, inquantum est Filius habens in se vere et perfecte naturam Patris — In-

---

blema estetico in Tommaso d'Aquino (Milan: Bompiani, 1982); English translation: *The Aesthetics of Thomas Aquinas* (Cambridge, Mass.: Harvard University Press, 1988). Here the author takes up again and evaluates his own doctoral thesis, published in 1956. On the scholastic understanding of art cf. J. Maritain, *Arte e scolastica* (Brescia: Morcelliana, 1980); regarding "art and beauty" see the discussion of the approach of St. Thomas, pp. 24ff. Regarding medieval aesthetics, E. De Bruyne, *Études d'esthétique médiévale,* 3 vols. (Bruges: De Tempel, 1946) is still valuable.

5. *Summa Theologica* Ia, q. 73, a. 1c.
6. L. Pareyson, *Estetica* (Turin: Edizioni di Filosofia, 1954), p. 284.

tegrity is proper to the Son, inasmuch as the Son has the nature of the
Father in himself in a real and perfect manner.

Thomas is too much a follower of the classical tradition not to recognize one particular element of truth that Greek culture handed on to
Christian thought: in matters of beauty, we are never content with a mo-
mentary appearance, with just a fragment. Beauty always points us to the
whole. The sense of *integritas* or *perfectio,* the fascination exercised over
Greek thought by the πάν, lives on in the ethos of the West. Thomas was
well aware of this, and had no difficulty in recognizing the Word as the
place of wholeness, knowing however that this identification radically
changes the way we think about the whole. Now the whole is no longer
hemmed round by unspeakable otherness. Now the whole is open, relational; now it is the place where each reality offers a welcome to the other
which is different, yet with which it is perfectly one.

This "open" whole expresses itself as such in two ways, which Thomas
indicates as being proper to the Word because he is the perfect icon of the
Father: the ways, that is, of *proportio* and *claritas.* By developing these two
aspects, Thomas is able further to clarify what beauty means for him:
beauty is really the Whole in the "perichoresis" of realities which are mu-
tually distinct, where these relate to each other in such a way that the Infinite becomes present in each of them. *Proportio:* the Whole is present in
that which is distinct from it inasmuch as the right proportion and harmony of the Whole is reproduced in the reality that is distinct. This is
beauty understood as "form," as harmonious relationships (so much so
that in Latin *formosus* means beautiful); this is Augustine's approach,
which in its turn carries forward the Greek tradition. If we were to general-
ize concerning Thomas's thought on the Trinity and Christ, we might say
beauty is to be found in the fragment which preserves in itself the relationship of the parts present in the Whole, reproducing this harmony in an
analogous way, form from form, measure from measure: "For Thomas
beauty . . . consists essentially in a condition of organic harmony."[7]

This, then, is the beauty of the incarnate Son: he is the *Verbum
abbreviatum* of the *Verbum aeternum,* the icon of what is unseen, the Word
which in our words offers a faithful echo of the eternal self-communication
of the divine Silence. *Proportio* "convenit cum proprio Filii, inquantum est

7. Eco, *Aesthetics of Thomas Aquinas,* p. 87.

imago expressa Patris. Unde videmus quod aliqua imago dicitur esse pulchra, si perfecte repreasentat rem" — Proportion "corresponds to that which is proper to the Son, inasmuch as he is the perfect image of the Father. From this we deduce that any image may be said to be beautiful if it perfectly represents/re-presents the object." The *re-praesentatio* of the Whole in the form of the fragment is achieved, that is, in a twofold sense: first, by "re-presenting" the proportions of the Whole, albeit in the absence of the complete Presence, and, second, by "representing" the harmony of the Whole, inasmuch as the fragment is a presence of an Absence which cannot in any case be represented. Thus the incarnate Word, the absence of the invisible and silent Father, points us back to the "beyond-ness" of the God with whom he abides in eternity, but at the same time he is that God's faithful presence, the nearness of the Absent One, the sacrament of the One in whom love has its source, and who is at one and the same time infinitely distant and infinitely near.

For Thomas, the other way in which the Whole makes its dwelling in the fragment, and so effects the event of beauty, is *claritas*. This is no longer a matter of the Whole rendering itself present and perceptible in the harmony of the parts: here the Whole bursts forth. Here the event of beauty is understood as a light shining brightly in the darkness of the night; here beauty shines through the fragment that offers no resistance:

> Essentially, "claritas" is the way the form communicates itself; it happens when the subject truly *sees* the object.[8]

Here the Whole is no longer simply understood as becoming present in the faithful reflection of its harmonious proportions; here it is perceived to be a light which shines forth, a deep abyss of splendor which opens before us and in which we are engulfed, or — in Trinitarian terms — the Silence whence comes the Word and which the Word makes us able to receive. This is beauty as *splendor,* beauty celebrated as brightness. This is beauty that breaks in upon us, a beauty which is glorious and overwhelming. Thomas perceives how this beauty came to be in the Son, splendor of the Father: *claritas* "convenit cum proprio Filii, inquantum est Verbum, quod quidem *lux* est, et *splendor intellectus*" — Brightness "corresponds to that which is proper to the Son, inasmuch as he is the Word, the *light* and *splendor* of understand-

---

8. Eco, *Aesthetics of Thomas Aquinas,* p. 119.

ing." Thus the Whole makes itself present in the Word not only in *integritas* and *proportio*, but also in *claritas*: not only in the harmony of the form, but also as a perfect reflection of the Father's glory, in a perfect circularity — typical of medieval thought — between "beauty" and "theophany."[9]

The Dialectic of Beauty

Thomas's approach to beauty thus brings together both Greek thought in its preoccupation with holding the multiplicity of realities together in the well-ordered depth of the One by the analogy of form, and the Judeo-Christian tradition with its faith in the living God who breaks into history like a consuming fire or a light shining in the darkness. With Thomas, these two traditions are drawn into a single movement in which the Other is welcomed and adored:

> For Thomas, beauty only happens in the interplay between ends; beauty lives as a moment of life, which tends towards perfection, and so towards God as the final and redeeming cause of everything that exists.[10]

The two aspects of beauty are distinct, and will constantly need to be brought into mutual interaction:

> Ad rationem pulchri . . . concurrit et claritas et debita proportio. — For a proper definition of beauty both splendor and due proportion are required.[11]

Form on its own is not enough, because it can lapse into mere aestheticism, the empty worship of the fragment considered in isolation from the Whole; but splendor alone, too, is insufficient, because the Whole breaks into time only by taking possession of a form and transfiguring it from within. Only thus does the fragment become a window onto the greater mystery, a place where eternity can appear in time.

The possible creation here of a separation — always lying in wait — between form and splendor indicates that Thomas's audacious synthesis is

9. See Eco, *Aesthetics of Thomas Aquinas*, pp. 6-7.
10. Eco, *Aesthetics of Thomas Aquinas*, p. 185.
11. *Summa Theologica* II IIae, q. 145, a. 2.c. Cf. also II IIae, q. 180, a. 3, ad 3um.

not without its risks. In particular, the gains he achieved by his approach to beauty would be completely misunderstood if we were to lose sight of the fact that the Mystery always remains transcendent; we would be entirely missing Thomas's point if we were to imagine that the Whole could somehow be absorbed in a single event, or in an object whose beauty is purely contingent and has no reference beyond itself. There is no room here for attributing absolute value to either splendor or form. No reflection on aesthetics that intends to maintain the divine nature of beauty can do without the analogical approach with its emphasis on the distance that endures in the forms of nearness. In this regard, Thomas proves to be a teacher without compare:

> Every time we speak about God we always do so in the context of analogy. Even properly to remain silent about God requires an analogical approach that achieves its end by staying quiet about its silence.[12]

When the things of God — including beauty — are the object of our concern, only the analogical approach allows us to overcome the potential incommunicability of total difference: this is because analogy draws into a single universe of meaning both the fragment and the Whole which makes itself present and perceptible in that fragment, while at the same time avoiding any loss of the sense of difference between the two. The common meaning shared by the fragment and the Whole is never taken to suggest that the two realities signified are in fact one and the same thing:

> This way of holding realities together lies in the middle between complete difference and mere sameness. In fact, in the things about which we speak by analogy there is not only one, single reason, as is the case with things which are the same; nor is there a totally different reason, as is the case with things which are different; here, instead, the name which is said in so many different ways signifies different proportions of relationship vis-à-vis one single reality.[13]

12. E. Jüngel, *God the Mystery of the World* (Grand Rapids: Eerdmans, 1983), p. 281. For an original and well-documented theoretical and historical reconstruction of the doctrine of analogy cf. V. Melchiorre, *La via analogica* (Milan: Vita e Pensiero, 1996).

13. "Iste modus communitatis medius est inter puram aequivocationem et simplicem univocationem. Neque enim in his quae analogice dicuntur, est una ratio, sicut et in univocis; nec totaliter diversa, sicut in aequivocis; sed nomen quod sic multipliciter dicitur, significant diversas proportiones ad aliquid unum." *Summa Theologica* Ia, q. 13, a. 5c.

The fundamental reason for the analogical character Thomas ascribes to beauty is the fact that it

> belongs in the realm of transcendentals, of those "passions or properties of being"... Unity, Truth, Goodness — which are but various aspects of Being... and which are, in actual fact, one with Being, and as infinite as Being itself, in so far as they are considered in their metaphysical reality. It may be said that Beauty is the radiance of all transcendentals united. Now the essential characteristic of transcendentals is the fact that they cannot be enclosed in any class; they transcend or go beyond any genus or category, because they permeate or imbue everything, and are present in any thing whatsoever.... Just as being is present everywhere, and everywhere diversified, so beauty spills over or spreads everywhere, and is everywhere diversified.[14]

It is because beauty pervades reality so completely that fascination with it has been almost spontaneously linked to the idea of the divine, which is omnipresent and sovereign:

> From this transcendental nature of beauty the ancients concluded that the attribute of beauty can and must belong to the Prime Cause, the Pure Act, who is the *supreme analogate* of all transcendental perfections; and that beauty is one of the Divine Names.[15]

These Names for the divine, which speak of God without in any way taking him prisoner, do no more than discreetly evoke that which lies beyond anything that can ever be said:

> Nothing our understanding can conceive of God succeeds in representing him, so that that which is proper to God himself remains hidden to us, and the highest knowledge we can have of him as we live out our journey here on earth lies in recognizing that God is above everything we can think of him.[16]

---

14. J. Maritain, *Creative Intuition in Art and Poetry,* Bollingen Series XXV, 1 (Kingsport, Tenn.: Pantheon, 1953), pp. 162-63.

15. Maritain, *Creative Intuition,* p. 163.

16. "Quidquid intellectus noster de Deo concipit, est deficiens a repraesentatione eius; et ideo quid est ipsius Dei semper nobis occultum remanet; et haec est summa cognitio quam de ipso in statu viae habere possumus, ut cognoscamus Deum esse supra omne id quod cogitamus de eo." Thomas Aquinas, *De veritate* 2, 1, ad 9m.

We find confirmation of Thomas's analogical understanding of beauty in the striking concordance between what he says about beauty's twofold reality and the two forms of analogy. In the one, indispensable struggle to speak of God, analogy travels two paths, much more closely interrelated than certain over-simplified schematizations might at first lead us to believe. The analogy of proportionality and the analogy of attribution are two ways of trying to say the unspeakable out of obedience to God's self-communication in creation and in his self-revelation in history. The analogy of proportionality gives the less inadequate expression to the immeasurable distance between the ultimate and the penultimate, because it focuses on the relationship between relationships; the analogy of attribution, concerning itself with the different levels of participation in a "unicum," underlines the continuity subsisting between the extremes (even though these are at an ever increasing distance the one from the other), a continuity which exists because of the unity of God's plan for, and action in, the world, as well as thanks to the mystery of the incarnation of God, in which the Eternal has himself made his own the words of time. To the hiatus emphasized by the analogy between relationships (or of "proportionality") must thus always be joined the correspondence, supposed by the continuity which makes it possible to attribute one single term to this-worldly realities and to God, in the unity of their universe of meaning and in the radical difference between the realities signified. Only by holding the two fields of analogy together does it become possible to maintain the every increasing difference between the this-worldly and the divine of which we are speaking, yet in a nearness which is all the same very great, instituted as it has been by God's own initiative: by turning towards human beings from the very beginning, God has made them constitutively capable of that encounter with grace which is salvation.

It is precisely in the similarity with these two forms of analogy that we can best understand the interrelationship between the two understandings of beauty in Thomas's thought: one might say that "form" is to "splendor" as the analogy of proportionality is to the analogy of attribution. While "form" expresses a similarity of relationships, where the harmony of the fragment images the harmony of the Whole, "splendor" evokes a participation made possible by the free and unpredictable irruption of the ultimate into the penultimate: here the open and welcoming Whole shines out in the provisionality and limitedness of time and space. If the need to reject any possible identity between Whole and fragment calls for a strong sense of

Transcendence, the no less necessary rejection of a total difference, and hence of their incommunicability, calls for a proximity between God and human beings in one context of meaning, and their mutual encounter in that mysterious place beyond words which is being itself: here the realities which exist and the words used to express them emerge in all their specific identity. It is not a simple matter of being uniting the divine and the this-worldly by way of different degrees of attribution, almost as if God were just one being among others, even if still to be considered the highest of all: but it is certainly in the dimension of being that God and his beauty make themselves accessible, and human beings can experience them, even if this happens beyond every determination of being, and thus in the holy Mystery which only lets itself be glimpsed in the event of revelation.

Thus it is that, on both the aesthetic and ontological levels, revelation understood as the event where God communicates and still conceals himself is the specific foundation for analogy: St. Thomas understands this well, when he goes beyond the logical evidence of difference in obedience to the fact that there exist statements of faith founded on the Word about God's coming.[17]

> To understand the gospel as correspondence means first of all to ask about the event which is the subject of the gospel. . . . the event of the correspondence of human talk to God is not a capacity of language itself; it is not its own possibility, but rather an alien possibility which is opened up to language and required of it.[18]

This way of understanding language's ability to speak of God holds together realities which are radically different, yet without lapsing into the idea that these realities are somehow the same; it maintains the unity of meaning which draws these realities together, even when one reality far surpasses the other, and is in some way radically discontinuous with it. The analogy of God's coming takes us beyond the incommunicability that would result from total difference: the universe of meaning within which God's self-communication to human beings takes place is one and all-encompassing,

---

17. "Propositiones affirmativae possunt vere formari de Deo. . ." *Summa Theologica* Ia, q. 13, a. 12. "Proposiitones quaedam affirmative subduntur fidei, utpote quod Deus est trinus et unus, et quod est omnipotens": ivi, *Sed contra*.

18. E. Jüngel, *God as the Mystery of the World* (Grand Rapids: Eerdmans, 1983), pp. 287, 289.

yet it also avoids any confusion which neglects real ontological difference, so that the realities signified are not simply "flattened," one on top of the other. Every expression of the *analogia Christi,* including beauty, offers this unity of meaning while preserving the infinite distance between the things signified: "form" is recognized as surpassed by "splendor," but as nevertheless necessary in order that the latter may shine forth without confusion.

Thus it is that, in the effort to offer a theological reading of beauty without forcing the divine into the straitjacket of this world, and without emptying the world of meaning as it is touched by the "consuming fire," it is precisely the way of analogy which offers a possible way forward: expressing the analogy of God's coming in the self-communication and self-concealment of the Word in the words of human speech, communication through beauty might represent the least inadequate way of speaking at the same time of the proximity of the infinitely distant God and the transcendence of his being, closer to us than we are to our own selves. This, among other things, is demonstrated in the extraordinary flowering of sacred art, especially in the Christian context. Because of its analogical character, the language of beauty must not be forced or bent to serve ends intent on saying things in an overly declaratory manner: the language of beauty must be respected in its capacity to evoke rather than to define, capable certainly of evoking life and ecstasy of thought and heart, but not automatically doing this. We need to be taught how to read the beautiful object: especially in the case of art that aims to express the divine, there is a real and proper discipline of the interpretation of Transcendence, the self-communication of a God who is perceived as ever greater in the veiled forms of his historical self-communication.

The Truth of Beauty

From Thomas's point of view, beauty may thus be understood as the Whole in the fragment, the totality of the divine Mystery revealed and hidden in the person of the incarnate Son. Seen in this way, beauty is the symbolic event that holds together both splendor and form, vision and speech both at rest and in movement out from themselves, the Christological analogy between the ultimate and the penultimate, proportionality and participation understood in terms of God's descent into the very darkness of Good Friday itself.

It is precisely at this point that we can lay hold of the deepest meaning of St. Thomas's approach to beauty, where, as has been said, his life's two worlds, the twofold wellspring of his intelligence and soul, meet. It is in the Word's being made flesh that Thomas perceives the irruption of the Other, the Silence of the Word becoming present and perceptible, to the supreme cry at the ninth hour, the ecstasy of the living God in love with his creatures. And it is here that Thomas senses that there must exist another relationship between the Whole and the fragment which surpasses the "Greek" approach of proportion and form, even as this was reworked from a Christian point of view by Augustine: Thomas senses a relationship that includes brokenness, scandal, and transgression.

His understanding of beauty here, where beauty is splendor in the sense of a light which shines out and envelops the beholder, no longer has its deepest origin in the Greek epistemology which has guided the destiny of the West, but in biblical, Judeo-Christian epistemology, where truth is not understood as ἀποκάλυψις, the removal of the veil to allow what was previously hidden to be seen; here, instead, truth is אמת (*'emet*), faithfulness, relationship. Where the privative ἀ negates the act of καλύπτειν, of hiding (corresponding to the Latin *lateo*), what is being expressed is a calling forth from hiddenness into the clear light of vision: this is the triumph of the idea (ἰδέα is connected to εἶδος = aspect, form, beauty, and to εἰδόν, which stands for ὁράω = I see: the Latin *video* comes from the same root). Truth ἀλήθεια — claims victory in vision: the Greeks *see* the truth; even from the depths of the dark cave they aspire to vision! When truth is so understood, as being exposed to vision, it will be conceived of as that "adaequatio" by which our sight embraces the object, the thing, in its totality. This is the epistemology which lies at the heart of Western philosophy, dominated, like the whole Western ethos, by the primacy of the idea, by that thirst for an all-encompassing vision which reaches its climax in the total embrace involved in Hegel's monism of the Spirit and in his ideological, totalitarian, and violent followers.

What is the consequence of this way of understanding truth for the idea of beauty? Truth as idea exhibits itself to sight in the beauty of the object, which is totally dominated by the gaze of the beholder. Beauty — understood as the presence of the truth which manifests itself — will thus be the Whole pinned down, as it were, in the fragment by a relationship of possession: beauty as form lets itself be seen, and offers itself to the total mastery of sight. The proportion of the parts, reflected in the eye which sees and transmitted to thought, is exactly what the Greeks meant by ἀλήθεια: the vision of beauty, truth as exact correspondence between the object and the mind in the all-encompassing act of the idea. Plotinus speaks for this tradition when he affirms that "the highest beauty lies in sight,"[19] adding that by the power of this vision those who contemplate beauty possess it and become beautiful themselves:

> If we have fixed our gaze on him who, dispensing beauty to all, remains motionless in himself, and offering all receives nothing for himself . . . what further beauty will we ever need? . . . original Beauty makes beautiful and lovable those who love it.[20]

Thomas was certainly an heir to this tradition, which is the great inspiring current of Western thought, the dynamo of its intellectual power, the expression of its soul athirst to dominate: for him, too, "beauty is that which pleases the sight, so that beauty consists in proper proportion."[21] On the aesthetic level, this is a reading of a beauty as unveiling itself, a beauty seen: this is beauty contemplated, before which we stand in awe. . . .

If in the Greek understanding of truth it is the One Alone which dominates, in the Hebrew approach to truth/fidelity, instead, first place goes to the Two, the covenant, relationship to another, because fidelity happens between the Two. Fidelity to oneself is mere consistency, repetition: only a twofold faithfulness, faithfulness to the Other, is the truth which frees and saves. In Judeo-Christian epistemology, then, truth stands originally for relationship: it is not you who sees the truth, but the truth which takes you to itself; it is not you who embraces truth as an idea, but you who listening and so let yourself be received by truth. Here it is not "cogito ergo sum" which triumphs, but "cogitor ergo sum": I exist because the Other thinks of me, because the Other receives and welcomes me, because the womb of Another is my dwelling-place — I live in a house which is not mine! The dwelling-place, the welcoming womb of the Other, is my-place-which-is-not-mine: more than seeing the truth, we must do it, dwell in it, and let ourselves be guided into all truth. . . .

Viewed within this perspective, what is beauty? No longer is it under-

19. Plotinus, *Enneads* I, 6, 1: "Of the beautiful."
20. Plotinus, *Enneads* I, 6, 7.
21. *Summa Theologica* I, q. 5, a. 4, ad 1um: "Pulchrum enim dicuntur quae visa placent. Unde pulchrum in debita proprotione consistit."

stood as the possession or domination of the object, albeit through vision: beauty here is understood as the tension, the event, the dynamism, the fire of a relationship between the Two. When this relationship happens, when the Other erupts into the fragment and touches it, and so shatters the shackles of an identity closed in upon itself — a form of identity which is always "bad" and enslaving — it is then that beauty is experienced. Thomas is too close to the biblical tradition for him too not also thus to conceive of beauty. But is this just one more example of *complexio catholica,* this time in the area of beauty? Is Thomas here just the usual theologian managing somehow to swallow everything, digest everything, and organize everything into unity? It might be so, certainly. Yet Thomas's endeavor to understand beauty by drawing together two epistemological worlds which are so different and distant from one another, holding them together in unity through the idea of the Whole present and perceptible in the fragment, is also something deeper and points to an encounter which had to be. The Greek tension between the One and the many is resolved here within the One itself: the divine Trinity is the origin, dwelling-place, and final keeper of everything it has called into existence. The Whole has made its home in the fragment because the relationship of love which constitutes it as purest beginning of all that is has now offered itself in the flesh: beauty is the ἀρχή of the Three, revealed in its highest form at the hour of the abandonment of the Cross, where the suffering of the crucified God opens the way into the depths of divine communion.

Here Thomas the Christian walks the way of the Trinity, which provides the fundamental perspective that pervades and characterizes his thinking, and which — to use the language of the moderns — makes it possible to describe the whole of his approach to beauty as a Trinitarian "aesthetic."[22] It is the kenosis of splendor in the form and the form of splendor in kenosis which is for him the event of the revelation of beauty which theology translates into thought and word: form and harmony, certainly, but also irruption, splendor, and life contemplated and possessed in vision, and, still further, death experienced to the extent of sharing in the infinite pain of the Cross. This is a theology of crucified love in a twofold

---

22. It is no accident that Thomas enumerates the three essential components of beauty "in his treatise on the Trinity, and this to demonstrate that beauty is not only a perfection of the divine nature, but must also be attributed, more appropriately, to the Person of the Son": Maritain, *Creative Intuition,* p. 163. The reference is to the texts quoted from the *Summa Theologica,* Ia, q. 39, a. 8.

sense: it is *theologia crucis* as well as *theologia crucifixa*, a word spoken about the abandonment of the Beloved, but also about the event which speaks of the experience of faith in him who tells us who he is when we as creatures go out of ourselves to meet and welcome him. In him, beauty is vision and repose; it is also hiatus, brokenness, and death; in him, above all, beauty is ἀγάπη. By Thomas's life, work, and eloquent silence, particularly of his final months,[23] Thomas teaches that these different moments, different souls, of beauty may never be taken in isolation one from the other.

Here we encounter Thomas as the faithful disciple of the incarnate Word, the Lord Jesus, in whom the Whole made its dwelling in the fragment once for all, drawing its every part towards the depths of divinity and journeying towards the works and days of human beings. Perhaps by thus pointing us to the fact that beauty as "crucified love" will always have a tragic dimension, Thomas leads us towards an even higher vision of beauty, which belongs to another time and place:

> Iesu, quem velatum nunc aspicio / oro fiat illud quod ta sitio: / ut, te revelata cernens facie, / visu sim beatus tuae gloriae — Jesus, whom now I see enveiled, / what I desire, when will it be? / Beholding your fair face revealed, / Your glory shall I be blessed to see.[24]

In these words, Thomas Aquinas offers us the example of a faith which has learned truly to recognize when beauty happens; he teaches us how to let ourselves be touched there by the holy Mystery, neither falling prey to the seductive draw of the penultimate, nor betraying the wonderful, albeit fragile, solidity of this passing world.

---

23. Cf. B. Forte, *The Silence of Thomas*, trans. D. Glenday (London: New City, 2003).

24. From the Eucharistic hymn "Adoro Te Devote" attributed to St. Thomas. English translation: *Devoutly I Adore Thee: The Prayers and Hymns of St. Thomas Aquinas*, ed. and trans. Robert Anderson and Johann Moser (Manchester, N.H.: Sophia Institute, 1993), p. 71.

Chapter Three

BEAUTY'S DEFEAT

Kierkegaard

The Necessary Insufficiency

threshold

It is the experience of beauty that leads human beings to the threshold, to that place where their limitedness is most acutely perceived, and where their yearning to go further is experienced with all the weight of life's contradictions. Thus it is that the aesthetic moment cannot be excluded from human existence, being indeed decisive: yet thus, too, it has to be surpassed. Here is born the supreme choice between despair and faith: and since without the former we cannot arrive at the latter, without walking beauty's path we will never arrive at the decision of faith. Beauty is the royal road to defeat; beauty is despairing, precious, terrible, and seductive! A Christianity deprived of beauty would risk being nothing other than a faith that has never known the darkness of despair, and so being an empty, tranquilizing, "established Christianity." On the other hand, though, beauty has its price: no one can pass through the fire and not risk being burned.

Only those who have accepted this risk and have stood firm in it can hope to accomplish the deeds of a "knight of faith": without a passion for beauty not even Abraham could have loved Isaac and been prepared to offer him in sacrifice on the holy mountain. True sacrifice requires love, and we only truly love a beauty that has stolen us from ourselves. And so there is a special strength and dignity in despair, only attained by those who have fallen in love with beauty, and absent from a this-worldly Christianity which has compromised with the calculations and comforts of this present age. Those who have experienced despair because of their experience of beauty have a nobility not known to the believing aesthete, who empties faith of its power and passion and turns it into a mere façade acceptable to the worldly-wise. Consequently, those who say clearly of themselves, "I have been and am a religious writer," have no hesitation in dedicating much of their best energies to the question of beauty,[1] without in any way compromising the truth of what they have said:

> If it is assumed that such a reader perfectly understands and judges the particular aesthetic work, he totally misunderstands me, since he does not understand it in the religious totality of my work as an author.[2]

The experience of beauty as the path that has to be walked to attain that despair which disposes us to make the leap of faith is described by Kierkegaard by means of an intricate network of different categories, states of mind, and figures which make their appearance throughout his "aesthetic cycle": the creative power of the imagination, the passion of desire, the calculated measure of seduction, all here join forces with melancholy, disenchantment, and defeat. This whole interwoven pattern of life-situations and feelings is described and examined with particular depth and detachment by Kierkegaard and his double, this latter being the pseudonym he from time to time employs. Against the abstraction of the then reigning Hegelian philosophy and its dialectic approach, Kierkegaard here aims to let concrete existence speak its truth: "Every movement of infinity is carried out through passion, and no reflection can produce a movement. This is the continual leap in existence that explains the movement, whereas mediation is a chimera, which in Hegel is supposed to explain everything and which is also the only thing he never has tried to explain."[3]

---

1. Kierkegaard himself lists the works which make up his aesthetic production in a note in *The Point of View for My Work as an Author,* in *The Point of View,* Kierkegaard's Writings VI, ed. and trans. Howard V. Hong and Edna H. Hong (Princeton: Princeton University Press, 1983), p. 29: *Either/Or, Fear and Trembling, Repetition, The Concept of Anxiety, Prefaces, Philosophical Fragments, Stages on Life's Way,* all written under a pseudonym. Alongside these works should be placed eighteen upbuilding discourses written under his own name.

2. *The Point of View for My Work as an Author,* p. 24. This primacy of the religious dimension in Kierkegaard is one of the reasons for the great influence exercised by him over Christian theology: cf. B. Forte, *Fare teologia dopo Kierkegaard* (Brescia: Morcelliana, 1997).

3. Søren Kierkegaard, *Fear and Trembling, Repetition,* Kierkegaard's Writings VI, ed. and trans. Howard V. Hong and Edna H. Hong (Princeton: Princeton University Press, 1983), p. 42.

Kierkegaard's critique of Hegelianism, however, does not imply that he fell into the Romantic net, even though Romanticism did exercise no little influence upon him. For him, Romanticism failed to pose the radical alternative he had so much at heart: Romantic pathos knows no real alternative between aesthetics and ethics, resolving everything as it does in an extreme form of subjectivism, where feeling and passion overwhelm the tragic seriousness of ethics and the yet more radical audacity of faith. For Kierkegaard, a new approach to beauty and to the experience of beauty has to be found between idealism and Romanticism, employing neither the shortcuts of dialectic thought nor letting itself be seduced by the heady attraction of mere states of mind. His use of a pseudonym is a very useful indicator of how he seeks to maintain a critical distance from the various positions he describes, while at the same time allowing him to express himself as both witness and expert.[4] Thus it is that, even if he still employs typically Romantic categories, such as irony, aestheticism, melancholy, and despair, they are never a point of arrival, but rather stages in the journey; they appear throughout the journey, but are never allowed to become the ultimate and absolute point of reference.

The aesthetic moment is thus one stage in the journey, as dramatic as it is decisive. As regards communication, this means that beauty can be a means of approaching truth, a way in which truth exercises its positive fascination. Kierkegaard writes:

> If you are able to do so, portray the aesthetic with all its bewitching charm, if possible captivate the other person, portray it with the kind of passionateness whereby it appeals particularly to him, hilariously to the hilarious, sadly to the sad, wittily to the witty, etc. — but above

4. Kierkegaard's originality and the unique significance of his aesthetic production receives enlightening treatment in A. Giannatiempo Quinzio, *L'estetico in Kierkegaard* (Naples: Liguori Editore, 1992). The young Th. W. Adorno, instead, in his *Kierkegaard. La costruzione dell'estetico* (Milan: Longanesi, 1983), seems more concerned with situating and interpreting Kierkegaard's aesthetics within the network of comparable thinkers. His approach highlights, on the one hand, the complexity of the very idea of aesthetics in Kierkegaard — which at various times covers the artistic experience, immediacy counterposed to the mediation of the ethical decision and the leap of faith, and the form of subjective communication (cf. pp. 47ff.) — and on the other he seems to lean toward a certain intellectualization of the aesthetic moment and its importance in Kierkegaard's work (even though Adorno in fact objects to such an assessment: cf. p. 284).

all do not forget one thing, . . . that it is the religious that is to come forward.[5]

This operation demonstrates the aesthetic fascination of Kierkegaard's writing, even if this is not without its risks:

No author is more cunning in his choice of words than Kierkegaard or aims at concealing more through his language than he who inexhaustibly denounced himself as a "spy in a higher service," part of the secret police, a dialectical seducer. There is no way to meet up with him in the fox kennel of infinitely reflected inferiority other than to take him at his word; he is to be caught in the traps set by his own hand.[6]

This latter assessment, however, would be justified only if aesthetics constituted a point of arrival for Kierkegaard: in fact, the constant preoccupation of his thinking was to employ aesthetics and journey through it as a stage which was at once both ambiguous and necessary. For him, all is lost if we are not brought to make the supreme choice:

What is the origin of evil? What has happened, not only to a given single individual but to humanity as a whole? It is intelligence that has seduced us and has overturned the point of view of Christianity. . . . As for everything else, it has been "both-and," "at the same time": it is *both* a certain thing — *and* Christian. . . . And what is it we now need? Nothing other than a disjunction: and *either — or* [*enten — eller*], so as to disentangle the whole thing. And this was probably my task.[7]

5. *The Point of View for My Work as an Author,* p. 24.

6. Adorno, *Kierkegaard,* pp. 41-42.

7. *Diario,* IX, 3705: X4 A 665. The third Italian edition of the *Diario* of S. Kierkegaard, edited by C. Fabro (Brescia, 1980-), has 12 volumes. The first reference given refers to this edition. The second reference is to the second edition of the Danish Integral Version which has 16 volumes in 25 tomes: *Søren Kierkegaard Papirer,* ed. N. Thulstrup (Copenhagen, 1968-70). This particular entry is not found in the English translation of Kierkegaard's diary and papers. See Søren Kierkegaard, *Journals and Papers,* 7 vols., ed. and trans. Howard V. Hong and Edna H. Hong (Bloomington: Indiana University Press, 1967-78). A general index (vol. 7) shows a concordance with the Danish Integral Version.

The Challenge to Move Forward

The aesthetic stage is thus destined to be surpassed, but this is no easy matter: beauty attracts and seduces. Even in religious experience, aesthetics abrogates the primacy to itself whenever the radical demands of imitation are replaced by the comforting attitude of admiration:

> What, then, is the difference between an admirer and an imitator? An imitator *is* or strives *to be* what he admires, and an admirer keeps himself personally detached, consciously or unconsciously does not discover that what is admired involves a certain claim upon him, to be or at least to strive to be what is admired.[8]

Thus Christ

> himself was fully aware of why his whole life on earth, from first to last, was designed solely to be able to have imitators and designed to make admirers impossible.[9]

So the task Kierkegaard sets himself is to move through and beyond the aesthetic stage and on into the imitation of the suffering Christ:

> it is so foolish . . . to want to reassure people about their eternal happiness, because, with regard to something in which the individual person has only himself to deal with, the most one person can do for another is to unsettle him.[10]

He senses that he should carry out this task by confronting the temptation to aestheticism found in established Christianity:

> In this world Christ's Church can truly endure only by struggling. . . . Established Christendom, where all are Christians but in hidden inwardness, in turn resembles the Church militant as little as the silence of death resembles the loudness of passion.[11]

8. Søren Kierkegaard, *Practice in Christianity*, 2 vols., ed. and trans. Howard V. Hong and Edna H. Hong (Princeton: Princeton University Press, 1992), vol. 1, p. 387.

9. Kierkegaard, *Practice in Christianity*, p. 238.

10. Søren Kierkegaard, *Concluding Unscientific Postscript to Philosophical Fragments*, Kierkegaard's Writings VI, ed. and trans. Howard V. Hong and Edna H. Hong (Princeton: Princeton University Press, 1992).

11. Kierkegaard, *Practice in Christianity*, vol. 1, p. 214.

w then may we escape beauty's snares and yet gather its most pre-
uit, the experience of limitedness and despair that prepares us for
the ɩᴇᴀp of faith? We are led to this critical point along three different but
converging paths by the three emblematic figures of the aesthetic experience: the poet, Don Giovanni, and the seducer.

The poet lives in the unresolved tension — proper to all literary activity — between the aesthetic moment and the ethical choice: in the production of artists such "duplexity from beginning to end,"[12] because though
they aim at the ultimate they are always somehow taken hold of by the
penultimate. In the passage of his *Diary* entitled "Confessions of a Poet"
Kierkegaard writes:

> His suffering is that he continually wants to be a religious individual
> and continually goes about it wrongly and becomes a poet — conse-
> quently an unhappy love affair with God (dialectical passion in the di-
> rection of there being something deceptive, as it were, about God).[13]

The poetic condition is thus marked by unhappiness, because poets
are lovers unable to attain the object of their love even though they yearn
for it with all their hearts; they are held hostages by their own desire for the
Eternal One, with no way of escape from the prison of time. They try flee-
ing into the world created by their imagination, but it is precisely here that
they are prevented from attaining ultimate and true reality: and so melancholy rules in their hearts, the melancholy which is nothing other than aes-
thetically experienced despair. In the *Diapsalmata,* which forms part of
Aut aut (Enten — Eller) and is the most significant part of Kierkegaard's
aesthetic cycle, he describes this situation in a deeply moving way: "Life for
me has become a bitter drink," "empty and meaningless," "an eternal
night."[14] Poets find life in memory and imagination, and hence in a condition of permanent inadequacy vis-à-vis reality, both the reality of daily
suffering as well as of ultimate suffering, which their hearts secretly yearn
for. Kierkegaard recognizes this poetic soul in himself:

---

12. The final quotation is from *The Point of View for My Work as an Author,* p. 29.

13. Søren Kierkegaard, *Journals and Papers,* vol. 1, ed. and trans. Howard V. Hong and
Edna H. Hong (Bloomington: Indiana University Press, 1967), entry 151.

14. Søren Kierkegaard, *Either/Or,* Kierkegaard's Writings III, ed. and trans. Howard V.
Hong and Edna H. Hong (Princeton: Princeton University Press, 1987), pp. 26, 29, 35.

In addition to my other numerous acquaintances, with whom, on the whole, I have a very formal relationship, I do have one intimate confidante — my melancholy, and in the midst of my joy, in the midst of my work, she beckons to me, calls me aside, even though physically I remain on the spot. It is the most faithful mistress I have known — no wonder, then, that I must be prepared to follow at any moment.[15]

So the creative work of poets is born of suffering, from the unresolved separation between the beloved and the possessed, between experience and expectation. While the Romantic influence is perceptible here, there is all the same no doubt that this sense of separation is a constant in Kierkegaard's life. Differently from Hegel, however, in him this "unhappy awareness" is not overcome through an operation at the conceptual level which unifies the divided ego in the serene possession of the idea; rather, it remains like a spring which continuously impels him towards the leap involved in the ethical decision and, above all, in the act of faith. The aesthetics of unhappiness, loving one's own pain, is not only the condition in which the wounded word of poetry is produced, evoking distant yet longed for horizons; it is also the fruitful stage of a journey which — impelled precisely by suffering — urges us to move forward in a decisive way. The ambiguous beauty attained by the unhappy poet is medicine for the soul in the measure that it calls out to that which lies beyond itself. . . .

Don Giovanni, the second figure to emerge in this journey into beauty, travels a similar route: here it is the power of desire that makes its appearance, in a restless pursuit of satisfaction and a permanent experience of dissatisfaction. From one conquest to another, hedonists repeat the tragic cycle to which their enslavement to desire condemns them: their lives are not founded on anything enduring, but on fleeting moments stolen from the Eternal One in the illusory ambition of somehow taking hold of beauty in final and complete satisfaction. It is music more than any other artistic medium which expresses the insatiability of desire: music, composed as it is of moments of sound in succession, offers the illusion of ecstatic fulfillment in the very act by which the sounds go inexorably to extinguish themselves in silence. Here Mozart was the great interpreter of Don Giovanni: through the power of his music, he was able to give incom-

15. Søren Kierkegaard, *Journals and Papers,* vol. 5, ed. and trans. Howard V. Hong and Edna H. Hong (Bloomington: Indiana University Press 1967), entry 5496. A similar text is found in "Diapsalmata" in *Either/Or,* p. 20.

parable expression to the joy of being alive, as well as to desire's tireless power and the tragic thirst which reappears ever anew after every apparent satisfaction.[16] If Don Giovanni is a perfect image of desire, which has "its absolute object in the individual," "desiring the individual absolutely," and so passing from one woman to the next in a constantly returning whirl-wind of desire-possession and dissatisfaction, the perfect image of Don Giovanni is provided by the succession of musical moments in the unity of the melody with its sense of a perfection inexorably in flight:

> The expression for this idea is Don Juan, and the expression for Don Juan, in turn, is simple and solely music.[17]

It is here that the true reality of the hedonist becomes clear, condemned never to be happy in the possession of what he deceived himself could give him happiness:

> In relation to enjoyment, he will find possibility more intensive than actuality.[18]

The bitter price the hedonist pays to his feverish desire is real anguish:

> Don Giovanni's life is not despair; it is, however, the full force of the sensuous, which is born in anxiety; and Don Giovanni himself is this anxiety, but this anxiety is precisely the demonic zest for life.[19]

If he could only move on to the ethical stage, the aesthete of pure pleasure would realize the tragedy of his condition: but his anguish can only prepare him for this leap, not force him to make it. The beauty pursued by Don Giovanni draws him to the threshold of the abyss: in this sense, it is precious. But to make the leap is an act that already surpasses the aesthetic moment, belonging as it does to the ethical and even more to the religious stages.

The seducer is the third figure to appear: if the poet's unhappiness

16. See the comment of Kierkegaard on Mozart's *Don Giovanni*: "The Immediate Erotic Stages or The Musical-Erotic," in *Either/Or*, pp. 47ff.

17. "The Immediate Erotic Stages," p. 85.

18. Quinzio, *L'estetico in Kierkegaard*, p. 142: the text quoted is from Kierkegaard, *Journals and Papers*, vol. 3, entry 3340.

19. "The Immediate Erotic Stages," p. 129.

arises from the distance between the beauty glimpsed by his imagination and the incompleteness of reality, if the hedonist's anguish is lived out in the frustration of his desire that remains unfulfilled precisely as he tries to satisfy it, the seducer's drama is lived out in the interplay between what attracts his interest and the word which both points to and denies this. Seduction's fascination lies precisely in drawing the object of his interest to himself without giving of himself: in it, the word is used to invite and inflame interest, but at the same time to act as a screen protecting him against the object invited. The seducer draws to him those who are far from him in order better to cause the pain of distance to emerge: "*Opposita iuxta se posita magis illucescunt.*"[20]

"The Diary of the Seducer," the most-read part of *Either/Or*, describes the passage from the domination of the sensual to that of the interesting: while desire begins as immediate but then becomes reflected, seduction begins as spontaneous and then becomes mediated. Here, beauty is as it were led within the individual: if the hedonist experiences a personal enjoyment of beauty, the seducer enjoys the beauty of his own personality. Pleasure here is falsified: it no longer consists in pursuing the prey to be possessed, but in contemplating oneself engaged in the sophisticated exercise of seduction, in the interplay between offering and refusing oneself. Precisely here, though, lies the seducer's drama: his calculations always overshoot reality, and so he always finds himself out of place, failing to grasp the moment and take the opportunity: "Most people rush after pleasure so fast that they rush right past it."[21] One can gain some insight here into Kierkegaard's personal experience in his relationship with Regina Olsen: he was able to draw her to himself; like no one else, he knew "how to bring a girl to the high point where he was sure she would offer everything," and yet it was precisely then that "he broke off, without the least overture having been made on his part, without a word about love having been said, to say nothing of a declaration, a promise."[22]

So in the heart of the seducer, too, dwells the bitterness of being cheated and abandoned. He is more in love with the seduction than with the person loved; he is focused on the play of his own ego more than on

20. Søren Kierkegaard, *Journals and Papers*, ed. and trans. Howard V. Hong and Edna H. Hong, vol. 4 (Bloomington: Indiana University Press, 1975), entry 4417.

21. Søren Kierkegaard, *Either/Or*, Kierkegaard's Writings III, ed. and trans. Howard V. Hong and Edna H. Hong (Princeton: Princeton University Press, 1987), p. 29.

22. "The Seducer's Diary," in *Either/Or*, Part I, pp. 301-445, here at p. 307.

the gift of himself to the other. As a consequence, he overshoots reality so as always to fall short of it. His game is his condemnation: his desire — mediated to him by his mind — is the springboard of his frustration, which no thought can succeed in mediating.

Thus it is that beauty draws back from those who love it: from poets, because for them it remains in the world of imagination; from Don Giovanni, because — reduced to the specific and flawed person to be possessed — it is never entirely satisfying; from the seducer, because — led within and reflected in the tricks of seduction — it is never laid hold of in free self-giving. And yet it is precisely thus that the aesthetic moment renders its service to the truth: the poet's unhappiness, the hedonist's anguish, and the seducer's failure make up that experience of limitation which renders evident the limitedness of every exclusively aesthetic experience and impels us towards the ethical and religious sphere. So it is that the journey into beauty leads to the life-giving moment of choice. . . .

Beauty Endures

For Kierkegaard, moving beyond the aesthetic stage means making a leap: the challenging choice must now become a decision. Aesthetics here have to stand aside to make way for what goes beyond them: the ethical decision and — beyond this again — the leap of faith. This decision arises from a perception of truth not as abstract certainty, but as invitation, offer, and absolute urgency:

> To objective reflection, truth becomes something objective, an object, and the point is to disregard the subject. To subjective reflection, truth becomes appropriation, inwardness, subjectivity, and the point is to immerse oneself, existing, in subjectivity.[23]

The aesthetic experience is limited inasmuch as the truth perceived in the concrete object can simply be contemplated and admired, without becoming something to live for, as instead is the case at the ethical stage:

23. Søren Kierkegaard, *Concluding Unscientific Postscript to Philosophical Fragments,* Kierkegaard's Writings VI, ed. and trans. Howard V. Hong and Edna H. Hong (Princeton: Princeton University Press, 1992), p. 192.

Only the truth that builds up is truth for you — that is, truth is inwardness, the inwardness of existence . . . in ethical definition.[24]

Ethics alone, however, are not enough: they do not yet open up to the Absolute, and so do not truly free us from the loneliness of the ego which continually tends to repeat itself. This, Kierkegaard tell us, is what is revealed in the lesson of Abraham, the "knight of faith":

If this duty [to God] is absolute, then the ethical is reduced to the relative. . . . God is the one who demands absolute love. . . . The absolute duty can lead one to do what ethics would forbid, but it can never lead the knight of faith to stop loving. Abraham demonstrates this. . . . He must love Isaac with his whole soul. Since God claims Isaac, he must, if possible, love him even more, and only then can he *sacrifice* him, for it is indeed this love for Isaac that makes his act a sacrifice by its paradoxical contrast to his love for God. But the distress and the anxiety in the paradox is that he, humanly speaking, is thoroughly incapable of making himself understandable.[25]

The difficulty of moving from the ethical stage to the leap of faith lies in the fact of having to face up to scandal (or offense):

"offense" [is] an altogether distinctively Christian term relating to faith. The possibility of offense is the crossroad, or it is like standing at the crossroad. From the possibility of offense, one turns either to offense or to faith, but one never comes to faith except from the possibility of offense.[26]

It is in this tension that the leap is made:

the leap . . . as the decision κατ' ἐξοχήν [par excellence] becomes specifically decisive for what is Christian and for every dogmatic category.[27]

To make this leap calls for the courage of responding to absolute paradox:

24. Kierkegaard, *Concluding Unscientific Postscript*, p. 245.

25. Søren Kierkegaard, *Fear and Trembling, Repetition*, Kierkegaard's Writings VI, ed. and trans. Howard V. Hong and Edna H. Hong (Princeton: Princeton University Press, 1983), pp. 70, 73, 74.

26. Søren Kierkegaard, *Practice in Christianity*, ed. and trans. Howard V. Hong and Edna H. Hong (Princeton: Princeton University Press, 1991), p. 81.

27. Kierkegaard, *Concluding Unscientific Postscript*, p. 105.

It takes a paradoxical and humble courage to grasp the whole temporal realm now by virtue of the absurd, and this is the courage of faith.[28]

this human being exists before God, may speak with God any time he wants to, assured of being heard by him. . . . Furthermore, for this person's sake, . . . God comes to the world, allows himself to be born, to suffer, to die, and this suffering God — he almost implores and beseeches this person to accept the help that is offered to him! Truly, if there is anything to lose one's mind over, this is it! Everyone lacking the humble courage to dare to believe this is offended.[29]

The singularity of the beautiful object, pervaded by the singularity of the Truth, the stumbling block of the unavoidable scandal of faith, does not leave thought and life untouched. Indeed, the concreteness of beauty points forward to the ethical stage and in the end to the leap of faith: *singularity,* indeed, holds the various stages of this journey together. It is there that beauty continues to shine out, as the Whole offered in the form and in the experience of the finite, and not in the all-encompassing suffocation of a system:

"The single individual" [*den Elkete*] is the category through which, in a religious sense, the age, history, the generation must go. . . . With the category "the single individual" I took a polemical aim at the system in the day when everything here at home was system and system — now the system is never mentioned anymore.[30]

For Kierkegaard, singularity is the decisive dimension of the truth about God and human beings:

"The single individual" — with this category the cause of Christianity stands or falls, now that the World-development has gone as far as it has in reflection. . . . As "the single individual" he is alone, alone in the whole world, alone face to face before God — then he will no doubt manage to obey.[31]

28. Kierkegaard, *Fear and Trembling, Repetition,* p. 49.
29. Kierkegaard, *The Sickness Unto Death: A Critical Psychological Exposition for Upbuilding and Awakening,* Kierkegaard's Writings XIX, ed. and trans. Howard V. Hong and Edna H. Hong (Princeton: Princeton University Press, 1980), p. 85.
30. Kierkegaard, *Journals and Papers,* entry 2004.
31. Kierkegaard, *Journals and Papers,* entry 2004.

radical singularity (margin annotation)

⟶ Revelation is nothing other than the self-communication of the Truth in the Single, the paradoxical offer of the singularity of Truth:

> The object of faith . . . is the actuality of the god in existence, that is, as a particular individual, that is, that the god has existed as an individual human being.[32]

Through the concreteness of singularity, the aesthetic moment continues to live in those stages of the journey that go beyond it, and especially in the religious sphere:

> The difficulty is to become a Christian, because every Christian is Christian only by being nailed to the paradox of having based his eternal happiness on the relation to something historical. Speculatively to transform Christianity into an eternal history, the god-in-time into an eternal becoming-of-the-deity, etc., is nothing but evasion and playing with words.[33]

In this sense, beauty is not only the other side of the poet's unhappiness, or of Don Giovanni's anguish, or of the seducer's defeat, but it is also that mysterious power which draws all towards the Single, the Unique, calling us to follow through the risky yet liberating decision of love:

> . . . died "of a longing for eternity."[34]

⟶ The day of faith is thus preceded by the night of despair, where the fascination of beauty has demonstrated its limit, and the pursuit of the other as something to be possessed has submitted to the supreme possibility of letting oneself be possessed by God, the only Consoler who conquers suffering and death:

> For "sorrow" is an old Word, almost as old as the World, but "the Comforter" is also an old word, yet still not quite as old, just as it does not become quite as old in the life of the individual even though he grow ever so old; there was always a night before the day, a night in which he vis-

---

32. Søren Kierkegaard, *Concluding Unscientific Postscript*, p. 326.

33. Kierkegaard, *Concluding Unscientific Postscript*, p. 578.

34. Quinzio, *L'estetico in Kierkegaard*, p. 99. The final quotation is from *The Point of View for My Work as an Author*, p. 97, where Kierkegaard imagines his own death.

ited Jesus (see Jn. 3:2) out of fear of the world, or a night when he doubted everything, when he found no stability between heaven and earth, a midnight — then Christ came as in days of old to the disciples through locked doors (see Jn. 20:19).[35]

Wherever there is an experience of anguish, the need for salvation is all the more urgently and acutely felt: "The anguished conscience understands Christianity. In the same way an animal understands when you lay a stone and a piece of bread before it and the animal is hungry."[36] Beauty is the mysterious path that leads to this salutary condition of neediness, to the deep darkness where despair dares to decide and its cry becomes a prayer. Precisely thus, beauty in all its ambiguity has a hidden saving power, and becomes an anticipation of the encounter with the Unique One who changes hearts and lives. . . .

either, or
commit / retreat

---

35. Kierkegaard, *Journals and Papers*, entry 4578.
36. Kierkegaard, *Journals and Papers*, entry 2461.

[Handwritten marginalia, top left:]

- morality & mystery
- moral decision
- tension (good/not good)
- concession to depths of mystery
  good & beautiful same
  ethics & aesthetics intertwined

Chapter Four
perpetual leap
- beauty @ the bottom
  perpetual promise of transformation

[Handwritten marginalia, top right:]

- Beauty & nihilism
- determination of identity in
  Infinite Good
- commitment – determine through choice
- tension – logic of double thought
- becomes ↑ difficult w/ sin involved
- beauty shines forth even in sin
- many faces
- the Suffering God
  - suffering that comes w/ choice
  - confront evil – Radical Question
  - infinite contradictions of Evil
- the Alternative Truth of Beauty
  - Christ – truth made individual
  - alt to nihilism
  - in christ, God takes evil & suffering
    into himself
- beauty – death & death
- @ work in sign of its opposite

[Handwritten marginalia, left side:]
impotence of God
conquers evil by becoming powerless
Beauty – embrace of contrasts
  overcomes in Christ
  frontier
choose beauty → end that approaches
appears in opposites – communication
  of final

TRAGIC BEAUTY

Dostoevsky

Beauty Will Save the World

Dostoevsky — "humanity's advocate"[1] — is one of the few who have perceived the relevance of beauty to the truest question of the human heart: redemption from evil, salvation victorious over death. It is to Prince Myshkin — the principal character in *The Idiot* and an enigmatic Christ-figure, the Innocent One who suffers for all[2] — that the young nihilist Ippolit, who is near to death, puts the decisive, terrible question:

> Is it true, prince, that you said once that "beauty" would save the world?
> . . . What sort of beauty will save the world?[3]

1. N. A. Berdyaev, "La rivelazione dell'uomo nell'opera di Dostoevsky," in *Un artista del pensiero. Saggi su Dostoevsky*, ed. G. Gigante (Naples: Cronopio, 1992), p. 50. The volume contains pieces by L. Šestàov, N. Berdyaev, F. Stepun, and S. Askol'dov. According to Berdyaev, "this is where his pathos is to be sought, this is what explains the uniqueness of his creative genius. In Dostoevsky there is nothing from outside human beings, all is revealed only in them, everything depends only on them" (p. 40). In what follows I also take up some of the ideas in my *In ascolto dell'Altro. Filosofia e rivelazione*, 2d ed. (Brescia: Morcelliana, 1998), pp. 112ff.

2. On Myshkin as a Christ figure cf. R. Guardini, *Dostoevsky. Il mondo religioso*, 4th ed. (Brescia: Morcelliana, 1995), pp. 271-323.

3. Fyodor Dostoevsky, *The Idiot*, trans. Constance Garnett (London: Heinemann, 1913), Part III, Chap. 5, p. 383.

The spectacle of suffering is such that no redemption may be sought in some sort of harmonious reconciliation smothering the scandal of the world's pain, especially when this pain touches us personally:

> What is there for me in this beauty when, every minute, every second I am obliged, forced, to recognize that even the tiny fly, buzzing in the sunlight beside me, has its share in the banquet and the chorus, knows its place, loves it and is happy; and I alone am an outcast, and only my cowardice has made me refuse it till now.[4]

This is why the beauty that will save the world must be different from all possible dreams and desires for superficial harmony:

> I admit that otherwise, that is, without the continual devouring of one another, it would have been impossible to arrange the world. I am even ready to admit that I can't understand anything about that arrangement. But this I know for certain: that if I have once been allowed to be conscious that "I am," it doesn't matter to me that there are mistakes in the construction of the world, and that without them it can't go on. Who will condemn me after that, and on what charge? Say what you like, it's all impossible and unjust.[5]

Without confronting its opposite — the scandalous spectacle of the evil that fills the world — no beauty will ever be able to save itself or others. Dostoevsky, a pilgrim along the winding paths of the human spirit, employs his logic of "double thoughts" to understand beauty too: by way of paradoxes pushed to the limit in which he marshals all his power to evoke the negation of good, he highlights

> the tragic contradiction and tragic movement that exist at the deepest level of the human being, where this movement and contradictions are immersed in the limitless being of God without however being dissolved in it.[6]

This also makes clear how beauty is under permanent siege from nihilism,

4. *The Idiot,* Part III, Chap. 7, p. 414.
5. *The Idiot,* Part III, Chap. 7, p. 416.
6. Berdyaev, "La rivelazione dell'uomo nell'opera di Dostoevsky," pp. 54-55.

a phenomenon which traverses his work like a dark power, like a temptation always on the point of striking, a prediction which has two kinds of fulfillment which are only apparently opposites: the violent, ecstatic, terror-laden revolutionary hypothesis, and the horizontal, disarming, unstable philosophical attitude expressed for the first time in Belinsky's formula: "Negation — that is my god."[7]

Dostoevsky thus demonstrates how beauty is constitutively inhabited by her opposite, at least in that tragic condition marked by the radical ambiguity introduced by sin, in which humankind is given to live in this world:

> Beauty ought to be reserved only for that which is valid, good, and true, and in a certain sense it is so — but the other aspect of beauty is also undeniable and disturbing, namely that it is not in fact so, and that it can shine forth in evil, in disorder, in indifference, and even in stupidity.[8]

This does not mean, however, that among beauty's many faces there is not still the flawless face of her origins, but this can only be recognized by those of pure and peaceful heart, like *Starets* Zosima or Prince Myshkin:

> In the sayings of the *starets,* the "beautiful" appears not only as the highest concept integrating all values but also as a reality which embraces the holy truth and the good that "people are thirsting for." How many are the faces of beauty! . . . And again its mystery finds in Prince Myshkin another voice, which seems to come from a time prior to sin yet which also knows sin. We might perhaps call it a voice from the kingdom in the Apocalypse. It sings of the eschatological beauty of the world redeemed, but a tremble from the memory of the past, of the "first" existence, with its suffering and evil, still sounds in it. . . .[9]

[margin handwritten note: the many faces of beauty]

The Suffering God and Beauty

It is precisely in the complex ambiguity of beauty's many faces that she throws down the radical challenge that no thinking person can avoid:

---

7. S. Givone, *Dostoevsky e la filosofia* (Bari: Laterza, 1984), p. 8.

8. Guardini, *Dostoevsky,* p. 289.

9. Guardini, *Dostoevsky,* p. 291.

For Myshkin the problem of God does not consist in how we attain him
or how we are sustained in him, but rather in how, coming from God,
we can bear to the last the fact of entering into and living within a world
of darkness and of sinful hardening, so different from God.[10]

The radical question of evil is thus presented as a permanent challenge
to the existence of a God capable of justifying ultimate and salvific beauty
and so of being the eternal and absolute truth of the world. The reasoning
here is both rigorous and terrible: if God exists, then the horror of the evil
devastating the earth is precisely that — devastating, infinite. But in fact
this horror *is* without end: hence, God exists. Yet at the same time the argument can be turned upside down: if there is a just God, where does evil
come from? But evil exists: hence, there cannot be such a God. To find a
way out of this dilemma, which seems entirely justified by the infinite contradictions of existence and by the radical ambiguity of beauty itself, there
is nothing other than a radical transformation of the idea we have of God
and of his beauty: only if God takes to himself the infinite suffering of the
world abandoned to evil, only if he enters into the deepest darkness of human misery, is suffering redeemed and death overcome. But this in fact
happened on the Cross of the Son: thus Christ is the overwhelming proof
of the truth which saves; he is indeed the alternative truth to the so-called
truth reason constructs for itself with its proofs. The singularity of truth,
the truth made flesh in a Single Being, identified in the person of the Son,
is as far as it can be from a theodicy of perfect harmonies: but this is what
Dostoevsky chooses, precisely as an alternative to the nihilist conclusions
of Western metaphysics:

> If anyone could prove to me that Christ is outside the truth, and if the
> truth really did exclude Christ, I should prefer to stay with Christ and
> not with truth.[11]

The suffering of Christ is a tremendous and awful event which succeeds
in explaining the tragedy of humanity only by extending the tragedy to
God. In this sense, useless suffering is exemplary: it is a case where evil is

---

10. Guardini, *Dostoevsky,* p. 311.

11. This passage is part of the letter written by Dostoevsky to Madame N. D. Fonvisin at
the beginning of March 1854; see *Letters of Fyodor Mikhailovich Dostoevsky,* trans. Ethel
Colburn Mayne (New York: McGraw-Hill, 1964), p. 71.

in God and therefore God must suffer. . . . When Dostoevsky highlights
the suffering Christ as the only possible response to the question about
the futility of suffering, he shows that he thinks that sorrow has a divine,
theogonic meaning. . . . A law of expiation burdens humanity with its
destiny of suffering; and into this tragic situation God's pardon comes
as an unexpected grace. But this pardon is possible in virtue of a tragedy
even greater than the human tragedy, namely the tragedy immanent in
God himself: the suffering of Christ and his abandonment by God.[12]

A truth which explains and organizes everything into a presumed universal harmony, the "apotheosis of awareness" of which Ivan Karamazov
speaks, is not worth its price: to the God of such truth Ivan himself "respect-
fully" returns the entrance ticket to his world. Only a truth that has passed
through the fire of its opposite and has let itself be licked by the flames of
nothingness, only *such* truth will save the world. As Alyosha replies to Ivan:

> Brother . . . you asked just now if there is in the whole world a being who
> could and would have the right to forgive. But there is such a being, and
> he can forgive everything, forgive all *and for all,* because he himself gave
> his innocent blood for all and for everything.[13]

Only from within, then, can nihilism be refuted: only from the darkness of
Good Friday, where God suffers and dies out of love of the world, is it possible to proclaim the victory of life and beauty, because that death is the
death of death.

Here in fact lies the tragedy which can never be excluded from our
knowledge of beauty: there is no access to the light except by way of the
Cross, no way in to life except through death. So faith has to pass through
the crucible of doubt, affirmation through the night of negation, and truth
must find a way through scandal and deepest darkness. That is how it was
for God, and so must it be too for his disciple:

> Divine suffering succeeds in being a complete expiation and liberation,
> in other words the final victory over evil and suffering, precisely because

12. L. Pareyson, *Ontologia della libertà. Il male e la sofferenza* (Turin: Einaudi, 1995), pp.
198-99. These are ideas that Pareyson had developed in *Dostoevsky. Filosofia, romanzo ed
esperienza religiosa* (Turin: Einaudi, 1993).

13. Fyodor Dostoevsky, *The Brothers Karamazov,* trans. Richard Pevear and Larissa
Volokhonsky (New York: Vintage, 1991), Part II, Book 5, Chap. IV, p. 246.

it is the moment of the greatest triumph of negativity, of evil and sorrow, which reach the point of mastering God; precisely because it is the
furthest point of the speedy human journey of negativity, beyond which
negativity has been unable to go and cannot go; and if this barrier of
least resistance has not been breached by the greatest assault, then
negativity has been overcome for ever and humanity has been delivered
from sorrow.[14]

The beauty that will save the world is revealed and at work in the sign of its
opposite:

It is extraordinary that the definitive victory over evil, suffering and de-
struction should be by God in his impotence, so impotent as to undergo
evil, suffering and death himself. It is extraordinary that in order to
show his omnipotence God should choose such an indirect and tortu-
ous way as that of his impotence.[15]

So beauty offers itself to us dwellers in time under the sign of ambiguity, at the frontier between being and nothingness, charged with tragic
power. The violent Dmitri says:

Beauty is a fearful and terrible thing! Fearful because it's undefinable,
and it cannot be defined, because here God gave us only riddles. Here
the shores converge, here all contradictions live together. . . . The terrible
thing is that beauty is not only fearful but also mysterious. Here the
devil is struggling with God, and the battlefield is the human heart.[16]

Choosing Beauty

If in this time of our mortal existence beauty is thus at work under the sign
of its opposite, it will not be so at the end: indeed, it is precisely the approach of the end that reveals hidden beauty. It might be said that time re-
deems eternity precisely because it passes with such inexorable haste: it is
death that confers on each present moment the depth of a wholeness and

14. Pareyson, *Ontologia della libertà*, pp. 202-3.
15. Pareyson, *Ontologia della libertà*, p. 203.
16. Dostoevsky, *The Brothers Karamazov,* Part I, Book 3, Chap. III, p. 108.

eternity which have been already attained; it is the approach of nothing-ness that makes us aware of the wonder of time, the joy of life. Only at the end will beauty be shown victorious:

> when the evil of the day is past and the future comes, then the future artist will find beautiful forms even for portraying the past disorder and chaos.[17]

For the present, the way to beauty is conversion of heart, the "gift of tears," of which *Starets* Zosima speaks:

> Nature is beautiful and sinless, and we, we alone, are godless and foolish, and do not understand that life is paradise, for we need only wish to un-derstand, and it will come at once in all its beauty, and we shall embrace each other and weep.[18]

For beauty to be manifested now, a moral decision is necessary, the choice made by a humble heart which is open to Mystery's depths: if in Kierkegaard the aesthetic and ethical remain separate stages in this jour-ney towards beauty, in Dostoevsky they are inextricably intertwined, in the interplay of "double thoughts." In this sense, there is a beauty even in the depths of the "underworld," which Dostoevsky has no hesitation in un-masking in his description of its torrid delights and confusion of the will, which so often go hand in hand with, and affirm themselves, in suffering:

> The feeling of delight was there just because I was so intensely aware of my own degradation . . . there was no escape, and that I should never become a different man; that even if there still was any time or faith left to make myself into something different, I should most likely have re-fused to do so.[19]

But it is precisely in this tragic affirmation of self, in this love for the darkness, where the experience of beauty is nourished by the most ardent enjoyments of despair, that nothingness makes its appearance:

17. Fyodor Dostoevsky, *The Adolescent,* trans. Richard Pevear and Larissa Volokhonsky (New York: Knopf, 2003), pp. 563-64.

18. Dostoevsky, *The Brothers Karamazov,* Part II, Book 6, Chap. IIc, p. 299.

19. Fyodor Dostoevsky, *Notes from Underground,* trans. David Magarshack, in *Great Short Stories* (New York: Perennial Classics, 2004), Part I, Chap. 2, p. 268.

We are stillborn, and for a long time we have been begotten not by living fathers, and that's just what we seem to like more and more. We are getting a taste for it.[20]

And it is here that the will to live imposes a moral change, an act of courage, which expresses itself in a decision that is open to the possibility of a beauty that saves:

It was clear that he must not now suffer passively, worrying himself over unsolved questions, but that he must do something, do it at once, and do it quickly. And he must decide on something, or else . . . or . . . accept one's lot humbly as it is, once for all and stifle everything in oneself, giving up all claim to activity, life, and love.[21]

The alternative faced by Raskolnikov is the supreme moral choice: either to abandon oneself to the triumph of nothingness, or react against it by way of uncalculating love. But this choice can only be made by those who have touched nihilism's despairing nadir: there expiation becomes possible, for those who place themselves before a God who himself entered the abyss as the supreme companion of human suffering and the supreme and merciful judge of the world's sin.

To make expiation means to wrestle with God. . . . The one who expiates and wrestles with God receives an incurable wound, because this is precisely what expiation means. . . Those who expiate impute that anguish to themselves, they take it into the depths of themselves, they inflict it on themselves, exactly as God inflicted it on himself. . . . To make expiation means staying within the contradiction — which is the same contradiction with which God is tormented and consigned to death. . . . Tenderness is for God, for God who suffers; but suffering is of God in an ultimate unsurpassable, tragic sense.[22]

If conversion of heart leads to recognition of the beauty which saves, and if the aesthetic way is thus joined to its ethical counterpart, the importance of freedom in Dostoevsky's world becomes particularly clear: it is

---

20. Dostoevsky, *Notes from the Underground,* Part II, Chap. 10, p. 377.

21. Dostoevsky, *Crime and Punishment,* trans. Constance Garnett (New York: Random House, 1956), p. 42.

22. Givone, *Dostoevsky e la filosofia,* pp. 123-24.

precisely in the area of freedom that the battle between nihilism and redemption is joined with special intensity, including with regard to the supreme value of beauty. In this sense, the legend of the Grand Inquisitor is a mighty apologia for the eternal conflict which makes human life essentially tragic: this is a struggle between the audacity of freedom and the consoling temptation of giving freedom up.[23] The Cardinal Inquisitor stands for all those who have sacrificed their freedom for the sake of happiness; Christ, who stands before him accused, is instead the champion of freedom won even at the price of happiness. The conflict between the two is irreconcilable: they represent the radical choice, which is hidden in every human heart and gives life its ineluctably tragic character. There is no middle ground between the two options, no conciliatory solution; the choice is stark and total:

> Man is a tragic being in that he belongs not only to this but also to the other world. For a tragic being who, like man, has eternity in himself, final organization, stability, and happiness on earth are possible only by renouncing the freedom and the image of God that are in him. Passing through the fire of all of Dostoevsky's tragedies, the thoughts of earthly man are translated into new revelations of Christianity. The legend of the Grand Inquisitor is a revelation of man, intimately bound to the revelation of Christ.[24]

This is why in the final analysis it is in the mystery of the crucified God that the deeply tragic nature of human existence is revealed to itself: if God has made death his own, paying the price of freedom to the last penny, here on this earth the way of the cross will always remain the way to freedom and beauty. Precisely because the eternal Son has drained the bitter cup to the lees, this way will always be the way to life, where beauty will be finally made known, never again to be hidden:

> "Karamazov!" cried Kolya, "Can it really be true as religion says, that we shall all rise from the dead, and come to life, and see one another again, and everyone . . . ?" "Certainly we shall rise, certainly we shall see, and

23. A complex interpretation of the Legend, "actualizing" it in terms of Russian and Western Christianity, is offered by V. Rozanov, *La leggenda del Grande Inquisitore* (Genoa: Marietti, 1989).

24. Berdyaev, *La rivelazione dell'uomo nell'opera di Dostoevsky,* p. 69.

gladly, joyfully tell one another all that has been," Alyosha replied, half laughing, half in ecstasy. "Ah, how good that will be!" burst from Kolya.[25]

What we await at the end of the long Good Friday that is the history of the world is the victory and glory of beauty. In order that this victory and this glory may come, though, beauty is and remains tragic, marked by ambiguity, and the place and object of struggle, choice, and submission. . . .

25. Dostoevsky, *The Brothers Karamazov,* Epilogue, Chap. III, p. 776.

Chapter Five

THE GLORY OF BEAUTY

Balthasar

Beauty Here and Now

The inspiration and starting point for Hans Urs von Balthasar's theological aesthetic is the fragment of Beauty constituted by the Cross of the eternal Son, the very summit of God's entire work of revelation. In fact, Balthasar had begun his work in this area from the Greek standpoint of the form of the beautiful, but he came to see that this approach was radically insufficient for the purposes of Christian theology, even though he also understood that the Christian theologian has a duty not to jettison the Greek tradition altogether. He moved from a preoccupation with how the harmony of beauty is manifested in the splendor of the form, to an awareness of the tragic character of the *mysterium paschale,* in which death is death both in the world and in God, but so that there may be fullness of life.

In this extraordinary journey of intellectual conversion, Balthasar traveled a similar path to Thomas Aquinas, while at the same time giving evidence of his own special speculative power and unique capacity for synthesis. It might be said that, for him, beauty is the "Whole in the fragment" *(das Ganze im Fragment)* in the strongest Christological sense that can be given to this expression: not the Wholly Other, separated and alien with respect to the fragment, nor the isolated and flawed fragment with respect to Whole, but the absent presence, the present absence, to which the expression points and which only the bright darkness of the Cross can in some measure illumine.

A text such as the following, chosen from among many possible examples, renders the idea in striking fashion:

> That Logos, in which everything in heaven and on earth is gathered and possesses its truth, descends into darkness, into fear . . . into an idéense which is the exact opposite of the truth-revealing nature of being. . . . The indicative has been lost; statements are possible only in the interrogative. The end of the question is a great cry. It is the word that is no longer a word. . . . Even the Logos, who assumed the form appropriate to him, must lose his shape. . . . God's Word in the world has fallen silent; he does not even ask in the night for God; he is laid out in the ground. The night that arches above him is no night of stars, but a night of dull distress and self-alienation in death. It is not a silence pregnant with a thousand secrets of love that come from the sensed presence of the beloved, but the silence of absence, of turning away, of empty abandonment, which comes after all the agonies of leave-taking.[1]

In speaking of how the Son was abandoned on the Cross, the language of love, which is also the language of beauty, evokes the unspeakable sorrow of supreme separation. . . .

It is precisely by dint of this singular equivalence between beauty and the abandoned Christ that Balthasar is led to perceive the intensely contemporary significance of beauty as the way to regain the sense of the true and the good in an age tempted to passive resignation and blind to those horizons which can provide life's foundation and meaning. His quintessentially Christian passion for the proclamation of the gospel is what impels him to focus on beauty with such intensity:

> Beauty is the word that shall be our first. Beauty is the last thing which the thinking intellect dares to approach, since only it dances as uncontained splendor around the double constellation of the true and the good and their inseparable relation to one another. Beauty is the disinterested one, without which the ancient world refused to understand itself, a world which both imperceptibly and yet unmistakably has bid

---

1. H. U. von Balthasar, *A Theological Anthropology* (New York: Sheed and Ward, 1967), pp. 279-80, 284. For the fundamental equivalence of beauty and Christological form in Balthasar cf. R. Vignolo, *Estetica e singolarità* (Milan: IPL, 1982).

farewell to our new world, a world of interest, leaving it to its own ava-rice and sadness.[2]

The dramatic and inevitable consequence of beauty being thus sent into exile is a loss of the sense of truth and goodness:

> In a world without beauty . . . the good also loses its attractiveness, the self-evidence of why it must be carried out . . . in a world that no longer has enough confidence in itself to affirm the beautiful, the proofs of the truth have lost their cogency.[3]

So it is that, in Balthasar's view, the most urgent need as the modern era reaches its close is for a Christianity which wins back the centrally im-portant transcendental significance of beauty with intellectual rigor: it is no longer enough simply to bear witness to God's otherness over against the world, even though such a task has proved both necessary and precious in so many periods of history. To a humanity that has discovered with such intensity the this-worldliness of the world, and pursued with such energy the project of emancipating itself from every form of dependence extrane-ous to the this-worldly horizon, it is more necessary than ever to propose God in human form, the at once fascinating and disquieting scandal of God's humanity: and this will mean rediscovering the aesthetic key to the whole Christian message.

> Only the one who loves finite form as the revelation of the infinite is both "mystic" and "aesthete."[4]

Only whoever has this sense of beauty — and hence of the paradoxical advent of the Whole in the fragment — can also truly proclaim a God who is significant for a humanity that has now become aware of the full dignity of the historical and the this-worldly. Only the explicit and reasoned awareness of this self-offering of the infinite in the finite, of distance in proximity, and thus only an aesthetic understanding of revelation and

---

2. H. U. von Balthasar, *The Glory of the Lord: A Theological Aesthetics,* vol. 1: *Seeing the Form* (San Francisco: Ignatius, 1982), p. 18. On Balthasar cf. E. Guerriero, *Hans Urs von Balthasar* (Cinisello Balsamo: Paoline, 1991), with bibliography.

3. Balthasar, *Seeing the Form,* p. 19.

4. H. U. von Balthasar, *The Glory of the Lord: A Theological Aesthetics,* vol. 2: *Studies in Theological Styles, Clerical Styles* (San Francisco: Ignatius, 1984), p. 114.

faith, will be able to speak effectively to this human, and at times "all too human," world of ours. Aesthetics are at one and the same time the way to give glory to the Eternal One in the miracle of his self-communication in the finite, as well as to proclaim to the world the joy of the salvation offered it in the *Verbum abbreviatum*.

In Search of Lost Beauty

Where and how will it be possible for modern thought — and those ship-wrecked with it — to make once again their own the saving path to beauty? Balthasar responds to this question by revisiting the language of beauty in the theological memory of the West, and recognizing there the expression of an ontological dialectic, which has left its mark on the whole history of beauty:

> Those words which attempt to convey the beautiful gravitate, first of all, toward the mystery of form [*Gestalt*] or of figure [*Gebilde*]. Formosus (beautiful) comes from forma (shape) and speciosus (comely) from species (líquenes). But this is to raise the question of the "great radiance from within" which transforms species into speciosa: the question of splendor. We are confronted simultaneously with both the figure and that which shines forth from the figure, making it into a worthy, a love-worthy thing. Similarly we are confronted with both the gathering and uniting of that which had been indifferently scattered — its gathering into the service of the one thing which now manifests and expresses itself — in the outpouring self-utterance of the one who was able to fashion by himself such a body of expression: by *himself,* I say, meaning "on his own initiative," and therefore with preeminence, freedom, sovereignty, out of his own interior space, particularity, and essence. Again, we are brought face to face with both interiority and its communication, the soul and its body, free discourse governed by laws and clarity of language.[5]

So what is said of beauty has a twofold meaning, and this points to a dialectic in the original structure of beauty itself: beauty is both form and splendor — the splendor of the form, and the kenosis of splendor. This original structure of beauty has its foundation in being itself, which both

5. Balthasar, *Seeing the Form,* p. 19.

reveals and conceals itself in its relationship with the world of beings. The ontology of beauty is nothing other than the translation into language of the twofold experience which these words about beauty express: first, the experience of taking possession of the form in the act of vision and, second, of being carried off towards the abyss in the irruption towards the finite of the infinite and immense.

So Balthasar describes this ontology of beauty in the manner of Thomas Aquinas:[6]

> We may, however, without prejudice distinguish and relate to each other, albeit in a very preliminary way, two elements in the beautiful which have traditionally controlled every aesthetic and which, with Thomas Aquinas, we could term species (or forma) and lumen (or splendor) — form [*Gestalt*] and splendor [*Glanz*]. As form, the beautiful can be materially grasped and even subjected to numerical calculation as a relationship of numbers, harmony, and the laws of Being. Protestant aesthetics has wholly misunderstood this dimension and even denounced it as heretical, locating the total essence of beauty in the event in which the light irrupts. Admittedly, form would not be beautiful unless it were fundamentally a sign and appearing of a depth and a fullness that, in themselves and in abstract sense remain both beyond our reach and our vision.[7]

The dialectic of beauty thus lies in a twofold relationship between the object that pleases and the subject it pleases. On the one hand, the Whole manifests itself in the fragment through an analogy of the relationships between the parts, and thus as a form which harmoniously reproduces the infinite in the tiniest of realities: here beauty can be contemplated and, as it were, embraced by sight. Thus "pulchra dicuntur quae visa placent,"[8] beauty is what pleases when it is seen. The Greeks had an unrivaled understanding of beauty from this point of view: for them, the beautiful object offers its complete inward harmony to the eye of the beholder, who finds a sense of deep repose in the heady delight of seeming possession. On the

6. Cf. Chapter 2 of this work and J. Maritain's particularly illuminating considerations in *Creative Intuition in Art and Poetry,* Bollingen Series XXV, 1 (Kingsport, Tenn.: Pantheon Books, 1953), pp. 160-67, a brilliant re-presentation of the theses of St. Thomas.

7. Balthasar, *Seeing the Form,* pp. 117-18.

8. Aquinas, *Summa Theologiae,* Ia, q. 5, a. 4, ad 1um.

other hand, in the beautiful object the splendor of the Whole breaks forth from the depths, enveloping those who contemplate it and bearing them off towards the unfathomable abysses it inhabits: here beauty can be desired, yearned for, invoked, attained, and sought ever anew. This is the modern understanding of beauty, the dominant approach in an age characterized by a growing awareness of the part played by subjectivity.

In the light of this twofold movement, which finds expression in words expressing the original ontological dialectic of beauty, Balthasar offers a rereading of the whole history of Western aesthetics:

> The form as it appears to us is beautiful only because the delight that it arouses in us is founded upon the fact that, in it, the truth and goodness of the depths of reality itself are manifested and bestowed, and this manifestation and bestowal reveal themselves to us as being something infinitely and inexhaustibly valuable and fascinating. The appearance of the form as revelation of the depths is an indissoluble union of two things. It is the real presence of the depths of the whole of reality and it is a real pointing beyond itself to these depths. In different periods of intellectual history, to be sure, one or the other of these aspects may be emphasized: on the one hand, classical perfection (volendung: the form which contains the depths), on the other, romantic boundlessness, infinity (unendlichkeit: the form that transcends itself by pointing beyond to the depths). Be this as it may, however, both aspects are inseparable from one another, and together they constitute the fundamental configuration of Being. We "behold" the form; but, if we really behold it, it is not as a detached form, rather in its unity with the depths that make their appearance in it. We see form as the splendor, as the glory of Being. We are "enraptured" by our contemplation of these depths and are "transported" to them. But, so long as we are dealing with the beautiful, this never happens in such a way [that we leave] the (horizontal) form behind us in order to plunge (vertically) to the naked depths.[9]

Even if Balthasar runs the risk of oversimplifying the undoubted complexity of the history of aesthetics,[10] his schematization has the merit of

9. Balthasar, *Seeing the Form,* p. 118.

10. A complexity which remains even in the shape of a heavily speculative and synthetic revisitation, as for example that by B. Croce in *Breviario di estetica* (Milan: Adelphi, 1990), pp. 119-48. S. Givone, *Storia dell'estetica,* 6th ed. (Rome: Laterza, 1996), presents the history of aesthetics as a "modern" discipline from a historical-critical point of view.

highlighting the different emphasis that distinguishes the classical understanding of beauty from the modern insistence on subjectivity. Both approaches to beauty certainly move in the ambit of the inevitable relationship between subject and object. Yet there can be no doubt that the classical approach accentuates the primacy of objectivity, and hence the harmony of the form, where the Whole inhabits the fragment through an analogy of proportionality. The modern approach, on the other hand, emphasizes the subjective journey implied in the aesthetic experience, not only from the subject toward the abyss of difference, but also from this abyss towards the subject who is, as it were, taken hold of and drawn out of himself or herself along the path of an analogy of attribution, which is not without its surprises and unexpected turns.

Both in the first and the second models, the dialectic of beauty liberates those who perceive this beauty from an asphyxiating imprisonment in the self. In the first case, it anchors them firmly in the objectivity — external to themselves — of the form of that which is beautiful; in the second, it projects them out of themselves towards the abyss of the Other in a never completely achieved movement of transcendence. Precisely because beauty has these effects, it has a salvific value: it opens us up to the power of objectivity, encouraging us to go beyond ourselves, and so we are led beyond the limits of a subjectivity imprisoned in itself, toward the shining generosity of the true and the good.

Needless to say, it cannot be taken for granted that all this will in fact happen: in Balthasar's view, beauty always offers itself to the beholder under the unsettling sign of ambiguity. In this ambiguity, being does indeed show itself but it also, as it were, conceals itself, and truth and goodness may be both perceived as well as paradoxically more deeply concealed. This is why it is a matter of urgency to identify the criterion that would allow us to recognize the movement of beauty and its authentically liberating and saving presence. Balthasar has no doubts as to what this criterion might be, and here his aesthetics differ as much from the classical speculation on the objectivity of the form, as they do from the modern adventure of subjectivity captured and overwhelmed by beauty. For him, it is the revelation of Christ which manifests beauty: in the Crucified and Risen One beauty offers itself as the Whole in the fragment, as much by way of the proportion of relationships, as by the journey of the subject to beyond the frontier, or the coming of transcendent otherness to the world of the subject. It follows from this that it is precisely theology that can build itself into a complete aesthetics, on condition that it is consistent with its object, which is the event of revelation, and so seek to propose itself not as an aesthetic theology, but as a theological aesthetic. . . .

A Theological Aesthetics

An aesthetic theology is one that succumbs to the attractions of subjectivity accepted as the absolute criterion:

> Man's habit of calling beautiful only what strikes him as such appears insurmountable, at least on earth. And therefore, at least practically speaking, it seems both advisable and necessary to steer clear of the theological application of aesthetic concepts. A theology that makes use of such concepts will sooner or later cease to be a "theological aesthetics" — that is, the attempt to do aesthetics at the level and with the methods of theology — and deteriorate into an "aesthetic theology" by betraying and selling out theological substance to the current viewpoints on an inner-worldly theory of beauty.[11]

We can note here the anti-modern polemic combined in Balthasar with an impassioned desire to dialogue with the culture of modernity so as to offer it the beauty that saves. Balthasar here expresses the strong reservations that the objectivity of an approach founded on the revelation of the transcendent and sovereign Other has vis-à-vis the elaboration of an all-encompassing system built on the absolute triumph of reason. Against every possible Hegelian "monism of the spirit," theological aesthetics insists on the ontological difference: it does not dissolve otherness in the triumph of identity, and does not absorb the solidity of beauty in just one further dimension of the closed world of subjectivity, even when this is understood as a phenomenology of the Absolute.

In Balthasar, however, the rejection of every possible aesthetic theology, and thus of the subjectivism which this would express, does not translate into extreme objectivism: modernity here has a positive influence on him, preventing him from setting against the imperialism of the subject a mere nostalgic return to the objectivity of ancient and medieval thought. Subject and object are to be appreciated in all the power of the tension

11. Balthasar, *Seeing the Form*, p. 38.

which holds them together, and which cannot be resolved by absolutizing either the one or the other: it is indeed precisely in the tension between these two poles that we can identify the place of beauty and the possibility of a theological aesthetic:

> When it comes to confronting the structure (in which we encounter all Being both objectively and subjectively) with the contents of Christian theology, it should be clear from the outset that there can be no question of a univocal transposition and application of categories. This must be so because the living God is neither an "existent" (subordinate to Being) nor "Being" itself, as it manifests and reveals itself essentially in everything that makes its appearance in form. Protestant theology, therefore, has been wholly right consistently to reject the application to biblical revelation of the schema inherited from pre-Christian, and especially Greek philosophy, a schema that distinguished between a "ground of Being" and an "appearance of Being." But we have already shown elsewhere that this schema exhibits different analogical gradations. . . . The creation, reconciliation, and redemption effected by the triune God if not his revelation in and to the world and man? Not a deed that would leave its doer in the background unknown and untouched, but a genuine self-representation on his part, a genuine unfolding of himself in the worldly stuff of nature, man, and history — an event which in a super-eminent sense may be called an "appearance" or "epiphany."[12]

It is thus in hermeneutical circularity between subject and object that the event of beauty comes to pass, with the necessary caveat, however, concerning the asymmetric character of this circularity: here the objective transcendent pole is the free and freely given origin as well as the final measure, and cannot be simply manipulated by subjectivity. The Other truly makes itself present and perceptible in the this-worldly fragment of its self-communication, but never entirely: here the divine does not simply hand itself over in this-worldly terms, but instead opens a window onto the unfathomable depths of the Eternal One. Understood theologically, beauty is the event of the absolutely free and unpredictable self-giving of the divine Whole in the fragment: the fragment really becomes the dwelling-place of the Whole, but the Whole does not simply become the fragment.

12. Balthasar, *Seeing the Form*, p. 119.

This powerful dialectic movement attains fulfillment and is made manifest in the event of the incarnation of the eternal Son, who is beauty in person:

> Just as we can never attain to the living God in any way except through his Son become man, but in this Son we can really attain to God in himself, so, too, we ought never to speak of God's beauty without reference to the form and manner of appearing which he exhibits in salvation-history. The beauty and glory which are proper to God may be inferred and "read" of God's epiphany and its incomprehensible glory which is worthy of God himself. But in trying to perceive God's own beauty and glory from the beauty of his manner of appearing we must neither simply equate the two — since we are to be transported per hunc (Deum visibilem) in invisibilium amorem — nor ought we to attempt to discover God's beauty by a mere causal inference from the beauty of God's epiphany, for such an inference would leave this epiphany behind. We must, rather, make good excessus to God himself with a theologia negativa which never detaches itself from its basis in a theologia positiva.[13]

So in Christ, the Crucified Christ, God journeys forth from himself towards his creatures, and at one and the same time it is possible in him for these creatures to journey away from self towards their Creator and Lord. It is here, in the encounter of these two asymmetric movements, that the event of beauty takes place in history, as the mysterious and veiled anticipation of that eternal beauty which one day will be fully manifest. The historical and this-worldly mediation of this eternal beauty emerges here in all its dignity and solidity: certainly, it will never be able to take hold of the infinite, which always transcends and surpasses this mediation, and yet it will nonetheless be indispensable if human beings are to open themselves to the silent, gentle, divine All, which has come to pronounce itself in the mediation, even if without, of course, saying all there is to say. The positive aspect of this theological aesthetic thus consists in its being rooted in the entirely historical words and events of beauty, which have been chosen by the sovereign and transcendent Eternal One as the path and place of his free self-communication. The "form" of Christ is the this-worldly measure which delineates and transmits the divine in its free self-offering to human

---

13. Balthasar, *Seeing the Form,* p. 124.

beings: the perception of this form *(Schau der Gestalt)*[14] is the certain space in which the glory of beauty can shine out, even if still in that darkness and provisionality characteristic of all that is experienced by those who dwell in time.

Balthasar applies the twofold key he has thus identified in the ontology of beauty to this decisive foundation for the perception of beauty, and thus arrives at what he considers to be the two fundamental areas of a theological aesthetic. On the one hand, such an aesthetic takes hold of the "form" in which the Other has pronounced himself and by doing so defines the conditions which make possible the exercise of a true human knowledge of the divine, with revelation as the starting-point. On the other, the theological aesthetic lets itself be taken hold of by the inrushing movement of beauty and so by the theological contemplation both of the *descensus Dei,* which is revelation and the gift of grace, as well as of the *ascensus hominis,* which is the salvation thus made possible.

> Theological aesthetics must properly be developed in two phases, which are:
>
> 1. The theory of vision (or fundamental theology): "aesthetics" in the Kantian sense as a theory about the perception of the form of God's self-revelation.
>
> 2. The theory of rupture (or dogmatic theology): "aesthetics" as a theory about the incarnation of God's glory in the consequent elevation of man to participate in that glory.[15]

It is thanks to this twofold operation that the theology of revelation, developed as a theological aesthetic, can make a well-founded claim to universality: transcending the Enlightenment's counterposing of the universal "truths of reason" [*Vernunfts-wahrheiten*] against the contingent "truths of fact" [*Geschichtswahrheiten*], theological reason, as reason open to the free irruption of Difference into the world of sameness, recognizes the *universale concretum et personale,* universal truth revealed in the Individual, which precisely in this way offers itself as the event of beauty, as the Whole in the fragment or infinitely tiny.

---

14. This is the title of the first volume of *The Glory of the Lord;* in English: *Seeing the Form.*

15. Balthasar, *Seeing the Form,* p. 125.

> The aesthetic experience is the union of the greatest possible concreteness of the individual form and the greatest possible universality of its meaning or of the epiphany within it of the mystery of Being. . . . In the Christian understanding . . . all impersonal or only half-personal categories of myth and philosophy have become wholly personal. . . . in Christ the *species* and the *lumen* coincide as manifest, personal love.[16]

Christ in person is truth and beauty, the advent of eternity in time, of the infinite into the finite; he is also the way in the opposite direction, to the salvation of humankind from finitude and death.

Thus, against the backdrop of a theological aesthetic thus formulated, salvation is seen to be both the subject's contemplation of the form, as well as the movement by which Beauty at one and the same time crosses the boundaries to take hold of those who contemplate and entrust itself to them. Inasmuch as the eternal All has now offered itself in the concrete reality of one Individual, who in the harmony of his being analogously represents the perfect encounter of the human and divine — "without confusion or change, without division or separation."[17] To contemplate Christ is to find peace in daring to gaze on Mystery. Mystery thus contemplated is the wellspring of all beatitude: here those who behold perceive the form of the Other and possess it in the vision of the Crucified and Risen One, but at the same time they are possessed and pervaded by the victorious glory which expresses itself in him. Inasmuch as the event of the Cross is a sacrifice — the act by which the Son hands himself over to the Father for love of the world (cf. Gal. 2:20) as well the act by which the Father accepts the sorrow of handing over the Son also for our benefit (cf. Rom. 8:32) — the beauty of the Abandoned One is "transgression": here the human subject is carried off toward the depths of the divine mystery and the thrice-holy God irrupts into human history and the heart of the believer.

> Seen with the eyes of faith, bliss and sacrificial abandonment are identical.[18]

---

16. Balthasar, *Seeing the Form*, pp. 234-35.

17. According to the ideas expressed in the dogmatic text of Chalcedon by the four adverbs which indicate the relationship between the human and divine natures in the one person of the eternal Son made flesh: cf. H. Denzinger and A. Schönmetzer, *Enchiridion Symbolorum*, 34th ed. (New York: Herder, 1967), n. 302.

18. Balthasar, *Seeing the Form*, p. 236.

So it is that the faith that saves is also the highest possible experience in this world of that beauty which conquers pain and death. In the believing response is reflected the first and last glory, which came to pitch its tent among us for our salvation: but this response is

> the reflection, not the glory itself. Put more precisely, she [the Church] is the response of glorification, and to this extent she is drawn into the glorious Word to which she responds, and into the splendor of the light without which she would not shine. What she reflects back in the night is the light of hope for the world.[19]

---

19. H. U. von Balthasar, *The Glory of the Lord: A Theological Aesthetics*, vol. 7: *Theology, the New Covenant* (San Francisco: Ignatius, 1989), p. 543.

Chapter Six

THE ICON OF BEAUTY

Evdokimov

A "Metaphysics" of Light

Pavel N. Evdokimov is an outstanding witness to how passionately the Orthodox East longs for the last things as they are anticipated and promised in the revelation of the crucified Lord. As in the whole great Eastern Christian tradition, in him too it is the light "of Tabor" which guides the theological enterprise, that light which shines from the mountain of the Transfiguration, where time's dark path is lit up by the splendor of the beauty from on high, perceptible only to the eye of faith.[1] In this kind of theological thinking, contemplation precedes and nourishes speculation, mystical experience founds intellectual activity, and doxology pervades and molds the exercise of the *logos:*

> For it is not knowledge that clarifies mystery; it is mystery that elucidates knowledge. We can know only because of realities we will never comprehend.[2]

The bright darkness characteristic of revealed mystery touches all things with the kiss of its light: in it, we are given to attain the hidden depths of all that exists.

---

1. Cf. P. Evdokimov, *La conoscenza di Dio secondo la tradizione orientale* (Rome: Paoline, 1969).

2. P. Evdokimov, *Woman and the Salvation of the World: A Christian Anthropology on the Charisms of Women,* trans. Anthony P. Gythiel (Crestwood, N.Y.: St. Vladimir's Seminary Press, 1994), p. 9.

This light, which shines forth from the depths of creation both as it first was and now continues to be, as well as from the riches of the redemption offered to every creature, holds together beginning and fulfillment, like a hidden web which keeps in existence everything that exists:

> The end and the beginning converse with one another beyond time. . . . This means that we must examine historical existence in the light of the Alpha and the Omega.[3]

There thus emerge the main lines of a true "metaphysics of light," in which all things find the place set aside for them both at their origin and in their destiny:

> The first day of creation . . . is not first but rather one, unique, not one of a series. It is the alpha which already carries within itself and calls forth its omega, the eighth day of the final harmony, the Pleroma. The first day is the joyous hymn of the Song of Songs sung by God himself, the fleshing eruption of "Let there be light" . . . the primal Light of "In the beginning," according to the absolute *in principio* is the most shattering revelation of the face of God. For the world just beginning its development, "Let there be light" means "Let the Revelation be" and "Let the one who reveals, let the Holy Spirit come!" The Father pronounces his Word, and the Spirit shows him forth; the Spirit is the *Light of the Word*.[4]

This light which shines from the abyss of the beginnings and of the eighth day is nothing other than a mysterious sharing in the life of God the Trinity, the womb and guardian of everything that exists: all things are created by the Father in the eternal generation of his Word, the Son, and the Spirit is the manifestation of this Word, the light shining from the Word, in which each of the creatures called to existence finds light.

The Trinity thus of itself pervades all things: everything is created in God, everything rests in his light, everything is immersed in the loving relationships between the Three, who create and sustain in being everything

---

3. Evdokimov, *Woman and the Salvation of the World*, pp. 13, 17.

4. P. Evdokimov, *The Art of the Icon: A Theology of Beauty,* trans. Fr. Steven Bigham (Torrance, Calif.: Oakwood Publications, 1990), pp. 6-7. On Evdokimov also cf. P. G. Gianazza, *Pavel Evdokimov, cantore dello Spirito Santo* (Rome: LAS, 1983), and O. Clement, *Orient-Occident. Deuz passeurs: Vladimir Lossky et Pavel Evdokimov* (Geneva, 1985).

that exists. The truth of all creatures is nothing other than their shining with the light of the origins, the bright beauty emanating from the intimate heart of their coming from, and dwelling in, the divine Trinity:

> To be in the Light is to be in an illuminating communion which reveals the icons of persons and things. This communion allows us to grasp their *logoi* as contained in divine thought and thus initiates these persons and things into their perfect wholeness, in other words persons and things are initiated that God willed for them.[5]

It is thus not knowledge that creates or "sees" light, but it is the light that comes from above which allows us human beings to see original truth and beauty, to share in the way God sees:

> The Taboric light is not only the object of the vision, but it is also its condition. . . . We are dealing here with the transmutation of man into light. His physical vision as well is changed, seeing things with God's eye; man's whole being is associated with this vision. It is in fact God who looks at himself in us.[6]

This Trinitarian "metaphysics" of light is not an arbitrary Eastern development of biblical revelation: on the contrary, according to Evdokimov it is founded on what is most characteristic in the identity of the Judeo-Christian tradition:

> It is generally believed that the Greeks laid greater importance on seeing while the Hebrews accentuated hearing. Israel is the people of the word and of hearing. But . . . in the messianic passages "Hear, O Israel" recedes into the background and "Lift up your eyes and see" takes its place. In other words, seeing replaces hearing. . . . In the Bible, the word and the image are in dialogue, they call to one another and express complementary elements of the one and the same Revelation.[7]

Since God entered history — to the point of pouring himself out entirely in the Incarnation of the Son and his paschal mystery — the visible has offered the invisible a home, even if without taking the invisible pris-

---

5. Evdokimov, *The Art of the Icon*, p. 7.
6. Evdokimov, *The Art of the Icon*, p. 233.
7. Evdokimov, *The Art of the Icon*, pp. 32-33.

oner, in a way at least analogous to how human words have been inhabited by the Word of God and by his Silence:

> The Invisible reveals itself in the visible: "He who has seen me has seen the Father." From the moment of the Incarnation, the image was to become an essential part of Christianity, on the same level as the Word.[8]

In the dialectic of revelation, however, in which the invisible offered itself as at one and the same time manifested and veiled by the visible, and the Word both spoke and was silent in human language, the *Orientale lumen* has accorded a special place to the manifestation of God over against his concealment: yet in this it has done nothing other than accentuate one of the possibilities contained in the form of divine self-communication itself.

> The Christian West mystically revolves around the Cross. . . . The Christian East . . . revolves around the Glory of God, triumphant over suffering and death.[9]

In all its expressions, the East emerges as jealous custodian and tenacious witness of the light coming from above. A high and eloquent sign of this is Eastern iconography:

> The theme of light . . . like a bolt of lightning . . . flashes across the sky of Orthodox iconography. It penetrates this art as though in its own natural element and transforms it into a grandiose "solar mysticism."[10]

As the East understands it, it is only by divine light that everything is truly illumined, and so it is only in that light that everything finds its true place and full meaning: the vocation and mission of human beings, the encounter with the God who saves, the Tabor-like anticipation offered by the icon, all these are nothing other than aspects and moments of this all-encompassing vision of the light from above. . . .

8. Evdokimov, *The Art of the Icon*, p. 33.
9. Evdokimov, *The Art of the Icon*, p. 171.
10. Evdokimov, *The Art of the Icon*, p. 299.

The Human Being: Thirst for Beauty

How then is the human being understood within this "metaphysics" of divine light? Evdokimov responds by employing the categories of a real "theological aesthetics":

> The power of divine love contains the universe and from chaos made it the Cosmos, that is Beauty. Normally every living thing reaches out and rises up toward the Sun of divine Beauty. . . . In his essence, man is created with a hunger for the beautiful; he is that very hunger . . . as "image of God" and being "of God's race."[11]

At their origin and in their most fundamental structure, human beings are a thirst for beauty, a thirst occasioned and kept strong by the "Light of the Word," who is the Spirit:

> The vocation of the Spirit is to be the Spirit of Beauty, the form of the forms. . . . in the Spirit we participate in the Beauty of divine nature.[12]

We creatures would, however, be unable to recognize this call of ours to beauty, as well as the work accomplished in us by the Consoler, if the image of the new human being had not been offered us in Christ:

> The face of Christ is the human face of God. The Holy Spirit rests on him and reveals to us absolute Beauty, a divine-human Beauty, that no art can ever properly and fully make visible. Only the icon can suggest such Beauty by means of the Taboric light.[13]

This anthropology of light — rooted as it is in the mystery of the Incarnation — in no way spiritualizes or circumvents the reality of the world: it is constructed in and for history, through sacramental events, which celebrate ever anew the irruption and presence of the divine in time:

> the "symbolic realism" of the liturgy which always signifies an *epiphanic* symbolism: what is invoked in the epiclesis answers by appearing imme-

---

11. Evdokimov, *The Art of the Icon,* p. 10.
12. Evdokimov, *The Art of the Icon,* p. 11.
13. Evdokimov, *The Art of the Icon,* p. 13.

diately, and this appearing shines in and through the visible aspects of the sacraments and the liturgy.[14]

And here one perceives the profound difference between Christian faith and Greek metaphysics: salvation *of* history, and not salvation *from* history, is what is proclaimed and accomplished by the "good news":

> According to Plato, the world of the senses participates in the idea by a diminution, loss of its own reality. It is but a shadow and pale reflection. . . . In the Bible, on the other hand, the more nature is firm, living, and full of vigor within the realm of its own value, the greater is its symbolic meaning. The more man is man, the more he is an image, an icon of God. The more man's person expands . . . the more Christ lives in him.[15]

The divine which has entered history does not compete with the human, but takes it up and exalts it, according humanity its full value precisely in its this-worldly and historical reality, directed to its final destiny in beauty and light.

Nor does this intense appreciation of the value of all that is this-worldly overlook the truth of the absolute primacy of the Transcendent: in this anthropology of light, God is and remains first, even when he offers himself as the friend and redeemer of humankind:

> The world is . . . *relative.* God is . . . *absolute.* To be relative is to exist in relation to what is not relative. It is uniquely in the iconographic relation to the absolute that the world finds its own reality as icon, similitude and likeness. Man could never have invented God; it is impossible to go toward God without having already gone out from him. Man can think about God because he is already inside God's thought; God is already thinking of himself inside man. Man could never have invented the icon either. Man aspires to beauty because he is already bathed in his light; in his very essence, man is thirsty for beauty and its image.[16]

So the truth about human beings does not originate in human beings: in their deepest being, they are made to receive the love that created them and that continues to renew them in the act of giving them life. What we

---

14. Evdokimov, *The Art of the Icon*, p. 14.
15. Evdokimov, *The Art of the Icon*, pp. 105-6.
16. Evdokimov, *The Art of the Icon*, p. 237.

have here is the exact opposite of the arrogant attitude found in Western modernity: here the subject as central character in the human drama is overwhelmed by the splendor of the light which alone gives human beings back to themselves. And this light comes to human beings, and shines on them and hence not from them, as the unique perspective of the icon:

> Perspective is often reversed in icons. The lines move in a reversed direction, that is, the point of perspective is not behind the panel but in front of it. It is the iconographic commentary on the gospel *metanoia*. The effect is startling because the perspective originates in the person who is looking at the icon. The lines thus come together in the spectator and give the impression that the people in the icon are coming out to meet those who are looking on. The world of the icon is turned *toward man*. Iconic vision is opposed to the dual vision of our carnal eyes. In iconic vision, the eye of the heart perceives the redeemed space that dilates into infinity and where everything rediscovers its proper place. While in the dual vision of carnal sight, our eyes see space according to the vanishing point of fallen space where everything is lost in the distance. The vanishing point encloses and closes everything up while the "approaching point" of icons dilates and opens everything up.[17]

Self-sufficiency destroys human beings: being humbly receptive to and grateful for the light, instead, raises them up and allows them to attain beauty, toward which their deepest being is destined to journey. . . .

The Coming of Beauty

The asymmetry of the relationship between the human and divine is also reflected in the movement that draws these two poles toward one another: God — light and infinite beauty — holds the initiative and the power, and brings about the fulfillment. And God always come first at all levels of his creatures' existence, especially at the constitutive and original level of their being.

> The beautiful is present in the harmony of all its elements and brings us face to face with a truth that cannot be demonstrated or proved, ex-

17. Evdokimov, *The Art of the Icon*, p. 225.

cept by contemplating. The mystery of the beautiful illuminates external phenomena from within as the soul radiates mysteriously on a person's face. The beautiful meets us and we know it intimately; it come close to us and begins to mould itself in the very likeness of our being. . . . An artist lends us his eyes so we can see a fragment in which the whole is nonetheless present as the sun is reflected in a drop of dew.[18]

The Whole dwells in the fragment by the power of a self-giving at the very beginning: human beings are called to recognize this divine self-giving, to welcome its mysterious presence, and let themselves be filled with the light shining from the paradox of the tiny Infinite.

To the reality of creaturehood as such is thus added the new and completely freely offered reality of redemption, in which human nature is raised to share in the life of God the Trinity:

God meets us, and he makes the ethical experience a vehicle for disciplining creation, and the aesthetical experience becomes an opening through which his beauty erupts.[19]

Above all, Christ is the place where Beauty came to shine among us in all its salvific splendor:

The beautiful, then, is as a shining forth, an epiphany, of the mysterious depths of being, of that interiority that is a witness to the intimate relation between the body and the spirit. "Ordered" and "deified" nature allows us to see God's Beauty through the human face of Christ.[20]

And so there opens up before human beings the impossible possibility of God, the paradoxical shining of light in darkness beyond every this-worldly premise or merit, the streams of living water flowing from deep within us, but whose source is elsewhere:

The paradox of the Christian faith is that it . . . makes history overflow its boundaries. At this point, it is not the way that is impossible but the impossible that is the way, and only the charisms can make it possi-

18. Evdokimov, *The Art of the Icon,* pp. 20-21.
19. Evdokimov, *The Art of the Icon,* p. 23.
20. Evdokimov, *The Art of the Icon,* p. 26.

ble. . . . That impossible way is the fiery eruption of the "totally other" coming from the depths of the world itself.[21]

All this shows forth Beauty, the perfect fulfillment of all things, in which every part finds its proper place and is able to be fully itself in flawless harmony with all the others:

> We are in the presence of Beauty, not when there is nothing more to add but when there is nothing left to take away, for Beauty is without limit, but it cannot accept to be in the presence of non-Beauty.[22]

This brightness of Beauty is the new life of the encounter with the living God, which does not only concern the exterior world, but gives a special place to intimacy and depth, a light shining out from there as if transforming the one who receives the light into a new source of light:

> The beauty of Greek aesthetics is, however, static harmony, being only on the surface. The Christian vision, on the other hand, is turned toward an interior dynamism, toward the sense of the divine in the infinite, for God's beauty is not measurable and transcends all attempts to subordinate it to rules. God's beauty goes beyond all forms and creates its own form. This is why a human form that is "too perfect" can be an obstacle.[23]

In sum, God does not love us because we are good and beautiful, but he makes us good and beautiful by loving us: it is not human perfection that merits the divine, but the superabundant generosity of divine light that transfigures even the most fragile humanity from within. The beauty of the Eternal One does not compete with human beings, even if it exalts precisely their apparently least beautiful quality: receptive humility, which alone is capable of entrusting itself to the Other once and for all. . . .

In this world of divine light shared with human beings the icon takes on its full meaning: the icon is the fragment that gives a home to the divine Advent, the tiny reality ready to receive the irruption of the infinite, the image of the impossible possibility which God comes to accomplish in the world.

21. Evdokimov, *The Art of the Icon*, p. 69.
22. Evdokimov, *The Art of the Icon*, p. 93.
23. Evdokimov, *The Art of the Icon*, p. 147.

Being a material point in this world, the icon opens a breach through which the Transcendent shines, and the successive waves of this presence transcend all limits and fill the whole universe.[24]

In the icon — contemplated in receptive silence — the asymmetry of the encounter between the human and divine shines forth and draws the beholder in:

The icon is the last arrow of human *eros* shot at the heart of the Mystery. . . . To the iconic arrow, the divine *Eros* answers with its burning but unspeakable closeness. Tabor shines but only silence discovers it.[25]

On the one hand, the icon is a song of praise and glory directed toward the divine:

An icon is the same kind of doxology but in a different form. It radiates joy and sings the glory of God in its own way. True beauty does not need proof. The icon does not prove anything; it simply lets true beauty shine forth.[26]

On the other, the icon is transparency of light, an instrument of the irruption of the Other and his Tabor-like splendor:

There is never a source of natural light shone on icons for light is their very subject, and we can never enlighten the sun. . . . The contemplation of the Transfiguration teaches the iconographer that he paints far more with light than with colors.[27]

It is thus not the subject who sees the icon or sees by means of it, but it is the icon which floods with its light all those who place themselves receptively before it, disposed to see what cannot be seen:

The icon is thus never a "window on nature" nor even a specific place but rather an opening onto the beyond, a beyond that is bathed in the light of the Eighth Day.[28]

24. Evdokimov, *The Art of the Icon,* p. 196.
25. Evdokimov, *The Art of the Icon,* p. 236.
26. Evdokimov, *The Art of the Icon,* p. 183.
27. Evdokimov, *The Art of the Icon,* p. 186.
28. Evdokimov, *The Art of the Icon,* p. 224.

For Evdokimov all this forms part of the deeper reality of biblical revelation, with the entirely new emphasis with which the East has learned to "pronounce" the unsayable Name:

> According to the Bible, God makes himself present in his name. An icon is God's name in a *drawn* form. In the pronounced name, through and with the icon, which "pronounces" it in a silent and visible way, our love carries us to venerate and embrace the grace of the real presence.[29]

And this is why it is Christ — the invisible God made visible, the incarnation of the Word — who is the true source of the icon's Tabor-like light:

> This art is raised from the dead in Christ. It is therefore no longer a sign or a painting but an icon; it is the symbol of a presence and its shining meeting place.[30]

The icon is a mysterious yet real sharing in the victory over the infinite distance created by sin, in the power of the redemption achieved by the Son who came in the flesh, who transfigures this flesh in himself and in us:

> For the Christian East, being deified is to contemplate the uncreated Light and to allow it to penetrate us. It is to reproduce in our very being the Christological mystery. . . . This is why the Lord's Transfiguration, the most brilliant manifestation of his light, plays such an important role in the mystical life of Orthodoxy. . . . The icon reveals to all the eschatological light of the saints. It is thus a ray of the Eighth Day, a witness of inaugurated eschatology.[31]

In order truly to read the icon we must thus share in the new life of the redeemed: it is only there that the eye of faith awakens and — purified in the Easter journey of the death and resurrection of Christ in us — is able to see the otherwise invisible.

> The icon is *a vision of things which cannot be seen.* Even more: it creates the transcendental and attests to its presence. It is a place of theophany, but it has passed through the Cross and death.[32]

29. Evdokimov, *The Art of the Icon*, p. 200.
30. Evdokimov, *The Art of the Icon*, p. 174.
31. Evdokimov, *The Art of the Icon*, p. 186.
32. Evdokimov, *Woman and the Salvation of the World*, p. 131.

The icon offers itself to the vision of faith while at the same time it teaches the soul to see:

> The state of grace enlightens us so we can see the light. The icon reveals that light to us all. The icon is prayer; it purifies and transfigures in its image those who contemplate it. It is mystery and teaches us to see in it the inhabited silence, heavenly joy on earth, and the brilliant shining of the beyond.[33]

In the encounter with the icon the unity of the divine plan shines out in maximum concentration: the gift "already" received in Christ and in the Spirit is offered as anticipation and pledge of the fulfillment "not yet" realized. Between the beginning and the end there is this Tabor-like light, condensed in the fragment where Beauty irrupts and draws to itself:

> The Alpha and the Omega meet, and the "let there be light" reaches its fulfillment in the "let there be beauty." On the Sophia icon, we can contemplate the *divine beauty* that saves. The unspeakable Kingdom and its vision overflow in the soul and allow us to have a glimpse of the light of the Eighth Day, in which the Holy Spirit will make Christ's humanity radiate like a "glass torch" shining with all the colors of the beyond. It will be the fiery icon of the Trinitarian glory.[34]

At the beginning and in the final fulfillment of all God's ways stands the beauty of Trinitarian love, shining with light: of this light, which transfigures the heart and history, the icon is a powerful presence, which invades and fascinates, dwelling in our ordinary days but with the splendor of celebration. In it — fragment pervaded by the All, tiny reality into which the Infinite irrupts — we are offered the dawn of the Kingdom which comes. . . .

---

33. Evdokimov, *The Art of the Icon,* p. 188.
34. Evdokimov, *The Art of the Icon,* p. 353.

Chapter Seven

THE MUSIC OF THE SPIRIT
Three Semantic Models

Can music be termed a "language"? If so, what does this language say and how does it say it? And to what extent can music become a "sacred" language, capable of mediating a dynamic movement of transcendence toward divine Mystery? If not, how then does it draw the hearer in?

Western thought has answered these questions in various ways.[1] Simplifying somewhat, we might say that the various affirmative responses follow one or another of three basic models: first, the "objectivist" or "cosmological" approach taken by the ancient world; second, the modern "subjectivist" or "anthropological" approach; and third, the contemporary, "semiological" approach. The negative response, instead, is most thoroughly systematized in the modern period in the "formalist" theory, propounded in a particularly lucid way by Eduard Hanslick.[2] Hanslick re-

---

1. Cf. E. Fubini, *L'estetica musicale dall'antichità al Settecento* (Turin: Einaudi, 1976) and *L'estetica musicale dal Settecento a oggi* (Turin: Einaudi, 1978), the latter with a wide bibliography; as well as A. Caracciolo, ed., *Musica e filosofia. Problemi e momenti dell'interpretazione filosofica della musica* (Bologna: Il Mulino, 1973), and G. Piana, *Filosofia della Musica* (Milan: Guerini, 1991), who sounds a warning about the complexity of the idea of music as a language and is critical of the possible reductionisms involved in any so-called "musical semiology": "Our criticisms regarding the semiological approach in no way exclude the use of the metaphor of language, but in fact allow us instead to employ this metaphor in a freely illustrative way, suited to each different context and with the necessary adaptation to the case under discussion" (p. 54). I presented the ideas contained in this chapter at Assisi on March 4, 1998, as an address to the Conference of the Italian St. Cecilia Association: I am grateful to the musicians and musicologists present for the enlightenment I drew from my exchanges with them.

2. Cf. Eduard Hanslick, *Vom Musikalisch-Schönen* (Leipzig, 1854); English translation:

jected the idea that the "content" of music is the expression of feelings, holding instead that music's beauty lies exclusively in the sounds themselves and the way they are related to each other:

> The ingenious coordination of intrinsically pleasing sounds, their consonance and contrast, their flight and re-approach, their increasing and diminishing strength — this it is which, in free and unimpeded forms, presents itself to our mental vision.[3]

Music is no more than an "arabesque of sounds," a "kaleidoscope":[4] always, but especially in the case of music, "the beautiful, strictly speaking, aims at nothing, since it is nothing but a form."[5]

The fact is, however, that if music were so to be understood, there would no longer be any question of whether it was capable of mediating a movement of transcendence, nor of the nature of any such movement — questions that instead do indeed arise as far as "sacred" music is concerned. This is why any consideration of whether the language of music is capable of expressing the sacred cannot but enter into dialogue with the various models intended to justify or explain music's semantic character. This, however, does not amount to any denial of the legitimacy of musical experiments and investigations inspired by the purely formalist approach. Rather, what is being said here is this: if a form of music defines itself as sacred inasmuch as it is produced and executed with the purpose of being open to and directed towards divine otherness, it will only be formally such when those producing or executing it understand it as a language capable of mediating a possible movement beyond itself and towards transcendence. "While affirming this, however, we are not excluding the possibility that such a transcendent movement [*excessus*] may in fact be produced beyond any sacred intentionality, or indeed that it might be held to be constitutive of music that it reveals 'the true meaning underlying it

---

The Beautiful in Music, trans. Gustav Cohen, ed. Morris Weitz (New York: The Liberal Arts Press, 1957).

3. Hanslick, *The Beautiful in Music,* p. 47.

4. Hanslick, *The Beautiful in Music,* p. 48. The influence of such ideas is to be found, for example, in Igor Stravinsky's music "with no subject," understood as pure formal equilibrium of sounds, "impuissante à *exprimer* quoi que ce soit," Stravinsky, *Chroniques de ma vie* (Paris, 1935), p. 116.

5. Hanslick, *The Beautiful in Music,* p. 10.

while conversely rendering it volatile and fleeting in the very act of reveal-ing it', thus revealing it as the non-revealable or inexpressible."[6]

Thus aware of the complexity of the matter in hand, here we intend simply to revisit the three semantic models already mentioned: albeit in different ways, they concur in understanding music as language. We will in particular seek to establish how capable they in fact are of demonstrating that music can communicate the sacred. This investigation will especially involve seeking potential similarities between the idea of music and of the Spirit, in conversation with thinkers who were at one and the same time theoreticians of musical beauty and proponents of a theology of the Spirit. If such an approach is possible for the first two models, given that we have Augustine as an interlocutor for the "objectivist" understanding of music and Hegel for the "subjectivist" approach, it is more difficult to establish the relationship between music, theology, and the experience of the Spirit within the parameters of musical "semiology." It is perhaps, however, pre-cisely this third model that opens up the freshest questions and challenges for the present and future creative power of "sacred" music.

The Heavenly Numbers

The "objectivist" or "cosmological" approach finds its most authoritative voice in Augustine's *De musica,* itself an heir to the theorizations of the classical world, and especially of the Pythagoreans.[7] Here music is under-stood as the highest expression of that orderly relationship of numbers on which the universe is founded, the purest echo of the "heavenly numbers." Augustine writes:

> Observe the heavens above and the bright things that shine there; ob-serve the earth below and the sea and all the things which walk, fly or swim therein: they have forms because they have numbers. Take these away, and they will be as nothing. (*De libero arbitrio* II, 16, 42)

6. V. Jankélévitch, *La musica e l'ineffabile,* ed. E. Lisciani-Petrini (Milan: Bompiani, 1998), p. 40. This is the central thesis of this interesting work, which is based on a deep awareness of the ineffability of the divine Name in the Hebrew tradition.

7. Cf. the edition with the Latin text on the facing page, edited by M. Bettetini (Milan: Rusconi, 1997). English translation in *The Fathers of the Church,* vol. 4, trans. Robert Catesby Taliaferro (New York: Catholic University of America Press, 1947), pp. 151-379.

Continuing the Pythagorean tradition, Augustine understands the numbers as the "ontological *a priori* foundations that determine the specific nature of all existent realities," so that "the difference between the numbers is the qualitative difference between these very realities."[8] Yet in Augustine this Greek approach is taken up into, and subsumed by, his own specifically Christian vision. For him, it is the Word who is *numerus — forma — species:* the ideal numbers are nothing other than God's thoughts, realities which exist inasmuch as they are thought by God in the creative act which he accomplished in and through his Son. The relationship between the numbers is thus no longer an order intrinsic to themselves — a kind of merely quantitative measurement of a mathematical kind — but originates instead in the "mind" of God, who determines the qualitative identity of each single thing that exists as well as its place in the whole.

In this way, the idea of creation radically transforms the Pythagorean and Platonic approaches. On the one hand, it points to an order which goes beyond the numbers, and, on the other, it introduces into the interplay between creating and created freedoms the possibility of disorder, of a rupture of the original relationship between the numbers, or, in other words — and using theological categories — the possibility of sin. Evil, be it physical or moral, manifests the presence of a disturbance which only freedom can introduce into creation. This is the origin of the dramatic ambiguity of all that exists: while in God's creative intention reality is regulated by a higher order, in its concrete, historical self-realization it is in fact shaken by disorder and woundedness.

Here we find the reason for the inherent ambiguity of Augustine's understanding of music. On the one hand, music, inasmuch as it is the ordered measure of numerical unities, mirrors the cosmic order intended by the Creator, and is the "ars bene modulandi" (*De musica* I, 2, 2), which imitates the *ratio* from which it arises by giving a *modus,* a precise measure, to each part of the whole. Thus understood, music elevates, because it leads the hearer into an awareness of the divine Logos of the world and, in echoing the cosmic order, is able to give expression to souls united in harmony before and in God. Gregorian chant is perhaps the most successful example of this way of understanding the language of music, an understanding that makes this form of chant a particularly appropriate way to encounter

8. W. Beierwaltes, "Augustins Interpretation von Sapientia XI, 21," *Revue des etudes augustiniennes* 15 (1969): 55.

the divine. In the orderly disposition of the sounds juxtaposed in a proper *modus*, the hearer is offered an outstanding mediation of transcendence, which places the individual and the community in a relationship of both imitation of, and participation in, the order conceived from before the ages in the eternal thought of God. Here music, moving from footfalls perceptible to the senses ("ab his vestigiis sensibilibus"), leads toward those dwelling-places where it is bereft of all that is corporeal ("ad ipsa cubilia, ubi ab omni corpore aliena est"; *De musica* V, 13, 28), and thus into a deep experience of beauty and joy:

> It thus cannot be denied that this discipline, if it is truly the science of good modulation, properly concerns itself with all movements which are well modulated and, above all, with those that have no reference beyond themselves, carrying rather in themselves the end of beauty and pleasure. (*De musica* V, 13, 28)

To the extent, however, that this order has been disturbed by the wrong use of freedom, music too can echo brokenness, and this not only in the sense of failing in modulation, and so an unsuccessful succession and inter-relationship of measures, but also and more deeply in the sense of confining itself to reproducing a superficial order, bound only to the senses and not molded on the more radical exigencies of the spirit open to the divine. This is the risk music carries within itself, and which Augustine describes in an eloquent and dramatic way: matter — the indispensable instrument for grasping the *ratio numerorum* — may seduce and draw toward itself alone, instead of pointing to that of which it is only a pale indicator.

> Since the body is mortal and fragile, it can only be dominated with great difficulty and much attention. As a consequence, the soul can risk making the mistake of giving greater importance to bodily pleasure, because matter submits to its attraction. (*De musica* VI, 4, 14)

Augustine bears extraordinary personal witness to this tension in his *Confessions*, where he tells how he had to struggle between the spiritual nourishment and consolation offered by music and song and the risk that in them the pleasure of the senses could prevail over inner delight:

> I realize that all the varied emotions of the human spirit respond in ways proper to themselves to a singing voice and a song, which arouse them by

appealing to some secret affinity. Yet sensuous gratification, to which I must not yield my mind for fear it grow languid, often deceives me: not content to follow meekly in the wake of reason, in whose company it has gained entrance, sensuous enjoyment often essays to run ahead and take the lead. . . . All the same, I remember the tears I shed at the Church's song in the early days of my newly-recovered faith, and how even today I am moved not by the singing as such but by the substance of what is sung, when it is rendered in a clear voice and in the most appropriate melodies, and then I recognize once more the value of this custom.[9]

Is it possible to identify some similarity between what Augustine has to say about music and his teaching on the Holy Spirit? At first sight, such a question may seem forced, but the texts instead offer it a striking response. It is well known that when Augustine reflects on the God of revelation, he devotes much space to the so-called psychological doctrine of the Trinity, based on the analogy between the divine life and the ways in which the human spirit knows and wills; yet this is not his only approach. He also travels another path, led by the central message of divine love. If God is Love, he says, the one and only God is not, and cannot be, alone: to love, there must be at least two, in a relationship so rich and deep between these two as to be open to another. The God who is Love is communion of the Three: the Lover, the Beloved, and Love received and given — the Father, the Son, and the Holy Spirit. To believe in this eternal Love means to believe that God is One in Three Persons, in a communion so perfect that the Three are truly One in love; it means, too, to believe that they are thus One in relationships which are so real, subsisting in the one divine essence, that they are truly Three in giving and receiving love, in mutual encounter and in openness to love:

You do see a trinity if you see charity. (*De Trinitate* 8, 8, 12)[10]

There you are with three, the lover, what is being loved, and love. (*De Trinitate* 6, 5, 7)

---

9. *The Confessions,* trans. Maria Boulding, OSB, ed. John E. Rotelle, OSA (New York: New City Press, 1997), pp. 269-70. Regarding this text cf. the theses of M. Poizat, *La Voix du diable, La jouissance lyrique sacrée* (Paris: Métailié, 1991).

10. English translation: *The Trinity,* trans. Edmund Hill, OP, ed. John E. Rotelle, OSA (New York: New City Press, 1990).

Therefore there are not more than three; one loving him who is from him, and one loving him from whom he is, and love itself. If this is not anything, how is it that *God is love* (1 Jn. 4:8, 16)? If it is not substance, how is it that God is substance? (*De Trinitate* 6, 5, 7)

The essence of the living God is thus this love eternally on the move: Love which loves, and goes out from itself; Love which is loved, and receives itself; and the Spirit of this Trinitarian love, which gives itself back and is infinitely open to the other in freedom. The essence of the Christian God is love in this eternal movement; it is the Trinity as the eternal story of love, which calls forth, takes up, and pervades the history of the world, the object of God's pure love.

Augustine does his thinking about the Spirit in the context of this eternal story of God's infinite freedom to love. The Third Person of the Blessed Trinity unites the One generated to the One who generates, showing how the indelible distinction of love does not mean separation: he is the communion between the Lover and the Beloved, and he also guarantees communion between the eternal Lover and his creatures, though not apart from the Beloved, but precisely in and through him. The Spirit ensures that unity is stronger than distinction, and that eternal joy is stronger than the pain caused by the non-love of creatures: he is the Spirit of unity, peace, and joy. The *vinculum caritatis* between the Father and the Son means that the distinction between them is taken up into the higher unity of the love which proceeds from the Father and, resting upon and reflected in the Son, returns to its origin without origin:

The Holy Spirit is a kind of inexpressible communion or fellowship of Father and Son (*ineffabilis quaedam communio*). (*De Trinitate* 5, 11, 12)

According to the Holy Scriptures this Holy Spirit is not just the Father's alone, nor the Son's alone, but the Spirit of them both, and thus he suggests to us the common charity by which the Father and the Son love each other. (*De Trinitate* 15, 17, 27)

In this dynamism of eternal love, the Father is, and remains, love's beginning, the Son its expression, and the Spirit the personal bond between the Two:

For whether he is the unity of both the others or their holiness or their charity, whether he is their unity because he is their charity, and their charity because their holiness, it is clear that he is not one of the two, since he is that by which the two are joined each to the other, by which the begotten is loved by the one who begets him and in turn loves the begetter. . . . So the Holy Spirit is something common to Father and Son, whatever it is, or is their very commonness or communion, consubstantial and co-eternal. (*De Trinitate* 6, 5, 7)

There is thus an analogy between, on the one hand, what music achieves by juxtaposing and melding the sounds in an orderly way, echoing the eternal order conceived by God the Creator, and what, on the other, the Spirit accomplishes in the unity and trinity of God: just as music is not something added to modulation but is the very modulation itself, so the Spirit is not extrinsic to God's relational life, but is the very relationship of love given and received by the Two:

Then why did he [the Apostle Paul] not mention the Holy Spirit? Was it perhaps because it follows that where one is mentioned cleaving to the other in such total peace that by this peace they are both one, this peace itself is to be understood, even though it is not mentioned? (*De Trinitate* 6, 9, 10)

Nor does this very deep unity worked by the Spirit annul the inner order of the Trinity's life; it instead respects this order so that unity does not annul difference, and difference does not destroy unity, similarly to how music does not eliminate the ordered concatenation of the notes, but is achieved precisely in that order, creating one melody from the different elements:

If the Son has everything that he has from the Father, he clearly has from the Father that the Holy Spirit should proceed from him. . . . But the Son is born of the Father and the Holy Spirit proceeds from the Father principally, and by the Father's wholly timeless gift from both of them jointly. (*De Trinitate* 15, 26, 47)

If the analogy thus glimpsed is not without foundation — granting the distance between the two terms in every analogical relationship, but also not annulling the relationship between these terms also highlighted by the analogy, one could say that music, inasmuch as it is the art of right modulation, is uniquely suited to evoking the Spirit's role as *vinculum caritatis aeternae*. It is thus not only the order of the heavenly spheres or of the world of ideas that music expresses, but — to the eyes of the Christian faith as understood by Augustine — the dynamic order of God's very life lived in relationship, and so also of those human lives which in the Church share in the communion of the Trinity. This would explain why the orderly progression and juxtaposition of sounds has provided such a successful vehicle for the sacred, as is witnessed, for example, by Gregorian chant and the sacred melodies of the East. In any case, the power of this analogy would lie in showing how music is a vehicle for the Sacred not only by giving expression to human feelings open towards the transcendent, but by relating the musical numbers to an orderly succession in time and scale which objectively evokes a higher order, that which governs the limitless dynamism of the relationship between the Father and the Son in the unity of the Holy Spirit.

The Feeling of the World

The "subjectivist" or "anthropological" approach understands music as an expression of the subject, and of its deepest identity, feelings, and affections, which in their turn become the voice of the more universal "feeling of the world." This understanding of music brought with it the imposition of tonal harmony, where a tonality established by the creative subject unifies the various shades of sound, in a process similar to that achieved by the use of perspective in the figurative arts, where the object is depicted in relation to the standpoint of the subject.

> Hearing the relation of sounds among themselves, between one sound which vibrates more rapidly and one which vibrates more slowly — that is, perceiving the connection between one which is higher and one which is lower, not only as a pleasing chord but also as a pure relation — and seeing in this relation a particular positive value, was an experience reserved to Western man. That which up till then had been read in an exclusively horizontal way, as a linear temporal sequence, suddenly acquired a new dimension: the vertical connections portended a depth of music.[11]

This "anthropological" understanding of musical language finds one of its most developed philosophical formulations in the work of G. W. F.

11. H. U. von Balthasar, *Lo sviluppo dell'idea musicale. Testimonianza per Mozart* (Milan: Glossa, 1995), p. 31.

Hegel and is also effectively described in the work of Arthur Schopen-hauer.[12] According to Hegel,

> this obliteration not of *one* dimension only but of the whole space, purely and simply, this complete withdrawal, of both the inner life and its expression, into subjectivity, brings completely into being the *second* romantic art — music,[13]

which thus

> forms the real center of that presentation which takes the subjective as such for both form and content.[14]

The spatial element cannot, however, be completely eliminated, because the language of communication by way of the senses always remains bound to space and time: this is why it

> consists here only in the fact that a specific sensuous material sacrifices its peaceful separatedness, turns to movement, . . . [and] vibrates itself. . . . The result of this mascillating vibration is sound or a note, the material of music.[15]

To this corresponds hearing:

> The ear . . . without itself turning to a practical relation to objects, listens to the result of the inner vibration of the body through which what comes before us is no longer the peaceful and material shape but the first and more ideal breath of the soul. Further, since the negativity into which the vibrating material enters here is on one side the canceling of the spatial situation, a cancellation cancelled again by the reaction of the body, therefore the expression of this double negation, i.e., sound, is an externality which in its coming-to-be is annihilated again by its very existence, and it vanishes of itself. Owing to this double negation of externality, implicit in the principle of sound, inner subjectivity corre-

12. Cf. A. Moscato, "La musica nel pensiero di Hegel e di Schopenhauer," in Caracciolo, ed., *Musica e filosofia*, pp. 93-118.

13. G. W. F. Hegel, *Aesthetics: Lectures on Fine Art*, 2 vols., trans. T. M. Knox (Oxford: Clarendon, 1975). Cf. esp. pp. 888-958.

14. Hegel, *Aesthetics*, p. 889.

15. Hegel, *Aesthetics*, p. 890.

sponds to it because the resounding, which in and by itself is something more ideal than independently really subsistent corporeality, gives up this more ideal existence also and therefore becomes a mode of expression adequate to the inner life.[16]

The lightness of sound thus becomes a metaphor for the deepest movements of the spirit, of that negation of negation by which it transcends its own bodiliness in the same act by which it takes that bodiliness to itself: in this way, the spirit is thus perceived as the only inner source and unifying principle of the subject's leading role.

It is in this fashion that music is seen to be the most appropriate way in which the spirit can express its inner life, and this in two ways. First, in music the spirit can show forth its original dialectic constitution: it continually goes beyond the bodiliness it has taken on as part of its ongoing life by taking that bodiliness into the higher inwardliness of the subject. Second, music lets the spirit express its inner movements, the relationships at work within its inner world, the world of affections and feelings:

> the proper task of music is to vivify some content or other in the sphere of the subjective inner life, not however for spiritual apprehension in the way that happens when this content is present in our consciousness as a general *idea*, or when, as a specific external *shape*, it is already present for our apprehension or acquires through art its appropriate appearance.[17]

Consequently,

> Inwardness as such is therefore the form in which music can conceive its subject matter and therefore it can adopt everything which can enter the inner life as such and which above all can be clothed in the form of feeling.[18]

Along these same lines, Arthur Schopenhauer, who sees the world as organized dialectically between the outwardliness of representation and the inwardliness of the will,[19] conceives of music as

16. Hegel, *Aesthetics*, pp. 890-91.
17. Hegel, *Aesthetics*, p. 902.
18. Hegel, *Aesthetics*.
19. Arthur Schopenhauer, *The World as Will and Representation*, 2 vols., trans. E. F. J. Payne (New York: Dover, 1958). See vol. 1, pp. 255-67.

a *copy of the will itself,* the objectivity of which are the Ideas. For this reason the effect of music is so very much more powerful and penetrating than is that of the other arts, for these others speak only of the shadow, but music of the essence.[20]

It is especially melody, the complex of sounds rhythmically and harmoniously organized into a musical form with a meaning of its own, which expresses the leading inward role of subjectivity, the world subjected to the power of the will: this, indeed, offers

> the uninterrupted significant connection of *one* thought from beginning to end, and expressing a whole. . . . Melody . . . relates the story of the intellectually enlightened will, the copy or impression whereof in actual life is the series of its deeds. Melody, however, says more: it relates the most secret history of the intellectually enlightened will, portrays every agitation, every effort, every movement of the will, everything which the faculty of reason summarizes under the wide and negative concept of feeling, and which cannot be further taken up into the abstractions of reason. Hence it has always been said that music is the language of feeling and of passion, just as words are the language of reason.[21]

In this light we can understand how the relationship between words and music has been upturned with respect to the characteristic approach of the ancient world: if for the ancients the eternal Logos expressed itself above all in the logos of verbal language, and only in a subordinate way in the modulation of the musical numbers, in Schopenhauer's vision it is to melody that the primacy must absolutely go:

> For this reason they [song and opera] should never forsake that subordinate position in order to make themselves the chief thing, and the music a mere means of expressing the song, since this is a great misconception and an utter absurdity. Everywhere music expresses only the quintessence of life and of its events, never these themselves, and therefore their differences do not always influence it. It is just this universality that belongs uniquely to music, together with the most precise distinctness, that gives it that high value as the panacea of all our sorrows.

20. Schopenhauer, *The World as Will and Representation,* p. 257.
21. Schopenhauer, *The World as Will and Representation,* p. 259.

Therefore, if music tries to stick too closely to the words, and to mould itself according to the events, it is endeavoring to speak a language not its own.[22]

Continuing to move in this direction, Schopenhauer is eventually led completely to upturn the primacy of objectivity, which characterized the ancient world and underpinned modal music, and to ascribe the primacy to subjectivity and the will:

We could just as well call the World embodied music as embodied will.[23]

The concepts are the *universalia post rem,* but music gives the *universalia ante rem,* and in reality the *universalia in re.*[24]

Compared to such an exalted notion of music, seen indeed as an effective anticipation of reality, Hegel's approach appears much more sober. According to him "we may not cherish a tasteless opinion about the powerfulness of music as such,"[25] and this because

it is only this subjective aspect in the actual production of a musical work that completes in music the significance of the subjective; but the performance may go so far in this subjective direction that the subjective side may be isolated as a one-sided extreme, with the result that subjective virtuosity in the production may as such be made the sole center and content of the enjoyment.[26]

Is it possible to identify in Hegel — as in Augustine — some similarity between his understanding of music and the way he presents the work of the Holy Spirit? For an answer, we can turn to his reflections in the *Lessons on the Philosophy of Religion,*[27] where he focuses on absolute religion, and more specifically on his considerations regarding the "kingdom of the Spirit." Here Hegel recognizes in the doctrine of the Trinity the highest ex-

---

22. Schopenhauer, *The World as Will and Representation,* pp. 261-62.

23. Schopenhauer, *The World as Will and Representation,* pp. 262-63.

24. Schopenhauer, *The World as Will and Representation,* p. 263.

25. Hegel, *Aesthetics,* p. 908.

26. Hegel, *Aesthetics,* p. 909.

27. G. W. F. Hegel, *Lectures on the Philosophy of Religion,* 3 vols., ed. Peter C. Hodgson, trans. R. F. Brown, P. C. Hodgson, and J. M. Stewart with the assistance of J. P. Fitzer and H. S. Harris (Berkeley: University of California Press, 1984-87).

pression of God as Spirit. He has, indeed, no hesitation in deducing the idea of the Trinity from the very concept of the divine. If God is Spirit, he says, he cannot but be knowledge: but in order to know, he needs to become an object to himself. It is thus that the original divine subject, the eternal Spirit, distinguishes himself from himself, objectifies himself, in order to know himself. This eternal process of self-distinction in God is the generation of the Word, of which the incarnation of the Son is the historical manifestation. But the process cannot halt at this painful separation: truly to know himself, God as Spirit must repossess himself in a unity higher than the original unity, so as to take into himself the separation and reconcile it. This third moment corresponds to the divine procession of the Holy Spirit and is revealed historically in the event of Pentecost, the gift of reconciliation and origin of the Church. The Trinity thus becomes the history of a unique divine Subject, who lives in himself — albeit in the highest way — the universal dialectical process of the Spirit in the three inseparable moments of the origin "in himself," of the objectification "for himself," and of the final synthesis "in and for himself":

> ["God"] is not to be grasped as a living God, as concrete content; it is not to be grasped as spirit. If "spirit" is not an empty word, then God must [be grasped] under this characteristic, just as in the church theology of former times God was called "triune." This is the key by which the nature of spirit is explicated. God is thus grasped as what he is for himself within himself; God [the Father] makes himself an object for himself [the Son]; then, in this object, God remains the undivided essence within this differentiation of himself within himself, and in this differentiation of himself loves himself, i.e., remains identical with himself — this is God as Spirit. . . . Thus it is just this definition of God by the church as a Trinity that is the concrete determination and nature of God as spirit; and spirit is an empty word if it is not grasped in this determination.[28]

For Hegel, it is in this light too that the rise of the Church can be rationally understood: what the Spirit accomplished in Christ, he accomplishes in Christians. The separate and distinct has been united: the divine idea, which has become a particularity, objectifying itself to the point of becoming an "immediate and present person," the man Christ Jesus, returns to its original identity. The risen Son is reconciled with the Father: but in him it

28. Hegel, *Lectures on the Philosophy of Religion*, vol. 1, pp. 126-27.

is the divine idea that reconciles itself with itself. Not only in him, however, are the subjective and the universal reconciled: thanks to the Spirit, every single individual can return to his or her original unity with God, every subjectivity can identify itself with the universality of the idea, in every disciple there can be a reliving of the infinite separation, surpassed and fulfilled in infinite reconciliation.

> The bond [of the disciples] . . . [lies] in the intuition of this speculative [element], the infinite love that comes from infinite anguish. . . . It is not for the [individual] the latter is nothing particular but, in regard to the idea, itself universal, but rather for [all] individuals, and *as thus actual in their subjectivity,* that the divine idea is spirit — the *Holy Spirit.* The Holy Spirit is in them; they are, they constitute, the universal Christian church, the communion of saints. Spirit is the infinite return into itself, infinite subjectivity. . . . This [is] the Spirit of God, or God as the present, actual Spirit, God dwelling in his community.[29]

The community is thus the fruit of the identification of each person with the whole, of the absorption of the individual into the universal, of the resolution of the subjective into the idea: thanks to and in the community, the Spirit lives in history and history is taken up into the divine:

> Thus the community itself is the existing Spirit, the Spirit in its existence [*Existenz*], God existing as community.[30]

The difficulty of, and resistance to, this process lies in the fact that the subject remains different from the absolute Spirit:

> There is still the external and deficient side of humanity: we commit errors; we can exist in a way that is not appropriate to this inward, substantial essentiality, this substantial, essential inwardness.[31]

This last consideration provides the starting-point for identifying the analogy between Hegel's understanding of the Spirit and what he says in his *Aesthetics* about music: here the note which is out of tune with the rest becomes a metaphor for the individual's resistance to the universal, and

29. Hegel, *Lectures on the Philosophy of Religion,* vol. 3, pp. 139-40.
30. Hegel, *Lectures on the Philosophy of Religion,* vol. 3, p. 331.
31. Hegel, *Lectures on the Philosophy of Religion,* vol. 3, p. 332.

harmony's victory over this resistance is like a living metaphor for the rec-onciliation of the individual with the whole of the Spirit in the Christian Church. Further, just as music can give the fullest expression to the sub-ject's harmonious inner life, the individual spirit, because it unifies in har-mony the different elements that compose that life, so in the eternal pro-cess which is the life of the absolute Spirit, there are different moments that are taken up into the dynamic unity of a higher synthesis. And as in God this higher *Aufhebung* is the Holy Spirit, so in music it is harmony it-self, understood as the unifying structure in which is expressed the leading role of the creative subjectivity of the musician and of all who enjoy the beauty of music. What then the Spirit accomplishes in the Church, consti-tuting her as the unity of different subjectivities in the one idea of the uni-versal concrete, who is the incarnate Word, tonal harmony accomplishes by melding the variety of the notes into the unity of the dominant melody.

In this light, music as understood by Hegel or by Schopenhauer, and so tonal harmony in general, becomes the special place where, on the one hand, the feelings of the individual subjectivities can find expression, and on the other it becomes possible for the subjective spirit to transcend itself into the higher unity of the absolute Spirit, of which it is in any case a phe-nomenology. It thus becomes possible to conceive of a sacred music that has the twofold effect of expressing the movement of transcendence of the human spirits towards the divine, as well as of their being drawn into the unity of the eternal Spirit, which historically is the Church. Modern sacred music, from sixteenth-century polyphony to the great Romantic and post-Romantic masterpieces, can be read entirely in the light of this analogy, which reveals this music's character as a privileged instrument of the expe-rience of the Holy Spirit in the community of the believers, united in the identification of each one of them with the whole, made accessible in the universal concrete, who is the incarnate Word.

The Music of Crisis

The "semiological" approach to music is especially common in our own day:[32] besides considering the message of music for what it is in its own ma-

---

32. Cf. J.-J. Nattiez, *Fondements d'une sémiologie de la musique* (Paris, 1975); Nattiez also edited various monographical issues of the review *Musique en jeu* dedicated to the theme:

terial reality, this approach situates it in relation to the strategies employed
in its production and in its assimilation on the part of the hearers. Such an
approach arises from a conviction of the inseparability of subject and object in the "hermeneutic circle," and hence from a realization of the continuous symbolic reference of all forms of human expression: this referential
movement passes from the material object, perceived as clearly as possible
in itself and in its internal organization, to, first, the "poietic" process of
which it is the result and, second, to the process of reception (sometimes referred to as "estesic") in which it comes to be configured in the world of the
receiving subject. With the theoreticians of "musical semiology," the "tri-
partite semiological scheme," composed of the object considered as the
starting point and then taking in its production and enjoyment, does not
begin from the hearer, but from the transmitter, and so focuses in the first
place on the active process of construction of the musical event. This does
not only imply the abandoning of any "formalism," by which the music
would only be justified or understood in itself and in the complex of its in-
trinsic forms; it also makes it possible for music to move beyond the restric-
tions placed on "musical beauty" both by the "numerical" understanding of
the ancients, as well as the harmonic approach of the moderns. As we have
seen, the ancients insisted that the art of right modulation must concern itself above all with ordering the successions of times and dimensions of in-
tervals ("servatis temporum atque intervallorum dimensionibus"; Augustine, *De musica* I, 3,4), the better to imitate eternal order. The moderns
instead placed great weight on reinforcing the relationship between "dominant" and "tonal," which founds the unity of the sounds and the interplay
of the chords. Atonality and dodecaphony thus postulate a free use of harmonic functions, fixed creatively in the "poietic" process by the artist himself, often subordinating the use of harmony to other parameters of language and to unusual means of production of the sounds. In a fine critical
revisitation of modern music, especially with regard to the work of Arnold
Schönberg and Igor Stravinsky, Theodor W. Adorno writes,

> Under the coercion of its own objective consequences music has criti-
> cally invalidated the idea of the polished work.[33]

Sémiologie de la musique (1971), *Analyse, méthodologie, sémiologie* (1973), *De la sémiologie à la sémantique musicale* (1975).

33. T. W. Adorno, *Philosophy of Modern Music*, trans. Anne G. Mitchell and Wesley V. Blomster (New York: Seabury Press, 1973), p. 29. On the meaning of the "break" effected by

Contemporary music thus appears to be experiencing a "crisis" which is a faithful reflection of the historical crisis experienced by the modern world in general: the totalitarian presumption of the ideological systems has produced the fragmentation and "shipwreck" of the so-called "postmodern." "Art would perhaps be authentic," adds Adorno, "only when it had totally rid itself of the idea of authenticity — the concept of being-so-and-not-otherwise" (p. 217): what perhaps is called for now, that is, is an art which is not ideological, not planned in the abstract, and which is free from every possible theoretical prejudice. However, even such a project could be turned into a form of musical totalitarianism if from the outset it refused any possible return to tonality: in fact,

> the advent of a new tonal system has not taken place. [. . .] Beginning from Schönberg's revolution, music has never stopped looking for solutions to the crisis of tonality.[34]

The most attentive representatives of musical semiology now have no hesitation in saying that "the time has come to seek and rebuild a new balance between the poietic and the estesic," which amounts to saying that

> while still refusing any nostalgic return to historically dated musical styles, a way must be found to reconcile contemporary music with the public.[35]

It has even been said that

> the tonal system has won the day by founding micro- and macrostructures on one and the same principle.[36]

So it would seem that in the area of music, too, the crisis of modernity has left the field, on the one hand, to experimentations of the most disparate kind, often with no stylistic coherence whatever, and, on the other, to some sort of search for a unifying context: this indeed is what in any case

---

Schönberg, a reflection of the wider crisis of the age, cf. M. Cacciari, *Krisis. Saggio sulla crisi del pensiero negativo* (Milan: Feltrinelli, 1976), pp. 99-142.

34. J.-J. Nattiez, *Il discorso musicale. Per una semiologia della musica* (Turin: Einaudi, 1987), p. 172.

35. Nattiez, *Il discorso musicale*, p. 175.

36. Nattiez, *Il discorso musicale*, p. 175.

may be said to have been happening in the more general history of culture at the end of the twentieth century. As far as music is concerned, such a unifying context, even if it is not so highly developed and all-encompassing as that regulated by the laws of harmony, nonetheless needs rules which make it a tool for communication, at the pain of rendering the production of music meaningless and reducing it to the sterile exercise of endless experimentation. Perhaps the challenge for modern music lies precisely in regaining a linguistic dimension that the "poietic" moment can share with those who receive the music thus produced, and which can thus reactivate the "hermeneutical circle," which in not a few cases seems to have been ruptured by experimental research.

Is it possible to seek some similarity between this situation of unease and, in many ways, of an apparently unresolved disruption, and an understanding of the Holy Spirit that may in some way find expression in it? Finding an answer to this question is even more problematic than in the two previous cases: in both of them, it was possible to turn to one particular thinker — Augustine or Hegel — to evaluate both a theory of music as well as a theology of the Spirit and the Trinity; this is not possible in the same way for the most representative voices in recent music. Even if at the risk of some arbitrariness, it is all the same possible to indicate a theology of the Spirit that might offer a theological model in which musical research too might find inspiration. While Western theology of Augustinian inspiration — concerned to stress the mysterious unity of the Christian God over against the Greeks' fascination with the One as separated and different from the many — underlines the Spirit's role as the personal bond of unity between the Father and the Son, the Christian East instead tends to highlight the Spirit's work as guarantor of openness in the relationship between the Father and the Son. The Paraclete here is perceived as the gift of love in person, and hence the outgoing movement of Lover and Beloved, their leaving themselves to give themselves to the other in eternity and time. Starting from the biblical witness, according to which whenever God moves out from himself in human history this happens in the Spirit — from creation (Gen. 1, 2) to prophecy, from the incarnation of the Word (Matt. 1, 18.20; Luke 1,35) to the birth of the Church (Acts 2, 11) — , this form of theology has laid great stress on the way eternal love goes out from itself in infinite self-offering. In this sense, the Spirit is seen as proceeding from the Father, the source of all divinity, through, by means of, and beyond the Son, as is seen in the work of salvation: the idea that the Consoler is the ecstasy and gift of God is expressed by the Greek Fathers with the very frequently recurring formula: "From the Father, through the Son, in the Spirit":

> This is a statement of the dynamism in which the Spirit is that in which — or the one in whom — the process is completed. . . . Here we have an economic order, but one expressing the order of the immanent Trinity. According to that order, the Spirit is the one through whom God's communication of himself is completed. His economic attributes are sanctification or the ability to make perfect. He is the completion . . . in the Tri-unity of God.[37]

Seen in this light, the Spirit is the superabundance of divine love, overflowing fullness, the generous, free, outgoing dynamism of bright communion: he is the creator Spirit, gift of the Most High, source and contagious fire of life (cf. the hymn *Veni Creator*). And in this same light the Spirit is an entirely new beginning, divine transgression, and creative freedom:

> The Holy Spirit breaks the possible sufficiency of the "face to face" relationship of the two prime figures. Christian Tradition has recognized in him a creative and dynamic role; in this sense, he is the one who gives rise to other differences. He is the openness of divine communion to that which is not divine. He is the dwelling of God in places where, in a certain sense God is "outside himself." That is why he was called "love." He is the ecstasy of God towards his "other": the creature. The third figure of the Trinitarian symbolism excludes the possibility of a "narcissistic" interpretation of the relationship between the prime figures: God is open, is communication, is the fount of life and of sharing.[38]

The fundamental consequence of this theological approach to the Spirit as exodus and gift is that the Word and the Original Silence, the eternal Son and the divine Father, do not exhaust themselves in one other: their encounter means neither imprisonment nor stasis, but openness, overflowing life, and dynamic, shining love. The special characteristic of their divine encounter is that it always remains open. It might be said that

---

37. Y. Congar, *I believe in the Holy Spirit*, trans. David Smith (New York: Seabury, 1983), p. 147.

38. C. Duquoc, *Un Dio diverso* (Brescia: Queriniana, 1978), p. 117.

the Spirit brings about in God the necessary condition for a love that is true — freedom from possessiveness and jealousy: "To love does not mean gazing into one other's eyes, but looking together towards one and the same goal," in the well-known words of Antoine de Saint-Exupéry. The "co-beloved" of the love of the Father and the Son, the "third" in the meeting of their reciprocal self-giving and receptivity, is, precisely in his distinction and personal consistency, the proof that eternal love does not enclose the Lover and Beloved in the circle of their mutual interchange, but causes them to meet in a fruitfulness which transcends both of them.[39] Their eternal encounter thus reveals the transcendence of eternal love, its free and generous turning towards the other, its nature as sharing, and so as source of personal self-communication, in the interplay of the relationships between the divine Persons, and in the way they relate to creatures, called into existence by them.

The eternal Spirit is thus the enduring openness and outgoingness of the Silence of the Father and of the Word: and as a consequence, he is the death of the Silence in the Word and of the Word in the Silence of ecstasy; he is, that is, the One who proceeds from the Father through the Son, living as the eternal self-communication of Silence and the silence of the Word, silent Word other than the Word that speaks, eloquent Silence other than the pure Silence of the Origin from which the Word proceeds. The Word spoken in time is not all that there is:

> But I tell you the truth, it is better for you that I go. For if I do not go, the Advocate will not come to you. But if I go, I will send him to you. (John 16:7)

The free and generous projection of the divine Mystery into history is not only Word, nor only Silence, nor simply both of these together. If it were only Word, it would not offer a way into the hidden depths of Silence; if it were only Silence, it would not be able to communicate with human beings, who are encountered through language. Even if it were Word *and* Silence together, it would still lack their mutual self-transcendence in the encounter effected by the Spirit: here the Word pronounces itself in the silence of this-worldly deeds transformed by the divine Advent, and Silence

39. In the Western Church Richard of St. Victor is the principal representative of this approach to the Spirit: cf. P. Cacciapuoti, *"Deus existentia amoris." Teologia della carità e teologia della Trinità negli scritti di Riccardo di San Vittore (+ 1173)* (Paris: Brepols, 1998).

is attained through the Word in contemplation of heart and in the dialogue of a life lived in God. To meet the Word is to be led into Silence and to listen deeply to it; to encounter Silence is to welcome the Word and live it out in the consistency of deeds.

Transposing this understanding of the Spirit to the musical event — produced, executed, and received — in the hope of discovering a possible analogy between the two, one can hypothesize a form of music in which interruption, transgression, and silence are no less eloquent than harmony and sound. It is a matter, that is, of arriving at a kind of music that — without excluding tonality *a priori,* but also without any rigid adherence to it — would be able to find expressive forms which could transmit the message of that openness, newness and freedom proper to the action of the Spirit in God and history. Such music — of which the works of Olivier Messiaen,[40] Krzysztof Penderecki,[41] and György Ligeti[42] might be considered examples — could in the context of an experience of the sacred serve to communicate the outgoing and liberating countenance of the divine mystery. There would thus be an analogy of language between the unforeseeable and unpredictable action of the Spirit, who blows where he wills, and the docile response to him of a believing heart and a community open to his work, without any hidebound attachment to the status quo or imprisonment in what has already been achieved.

Such music would certainly not transmit the classical idea of beauty

40. French composer and organist (1908-92), he developed a musical language in which traditional elements are melded with the techniques of serial music and sounds inspired by birdsong, in an overall context of a markedly religious concern in a Catholic perspective. Many of his works are inspired by the Scriptures, e.g., *Les corps glorieux* (1939), *Vision de l'Amen* (1943), *Trois petites liturgies de la présence divine* (1944), *La transfiguration* (1969). The oratorio *Saint François d'Assis* (1983) represents a synthesis of his mature work.

41. Polish composer, born in 1933, he superimposes musical techniques, ranging from Gregorian chant to dodecaphonic series, and from Renaissance to serial counterpoint, on the use of a variety of sounds. The religious inspiration of his work is explicit, as he himself declares: "It is enough simply to have a religious faith and to want to express it. I raise no objection against those who consider my music to be a profession of faith." Among his works may be noted his *Passio secundum Lucam* (1962-65), *Dies irae* (1967), and *Polish Requiem* (1984).

42. Born in Transylvania in 1923, he went on to become an Austrian citizen. His work is distinguished by the search for the frontier between sound and noise, with a taste for discrepancy and distance and a predilection for asymmetries and asynchronies, without, however, excluding some use of harmony. Among his works of religious inspiration may be noted his *Requiem* (1965) and the chorale for sixteen voices a cappella *Lux aeterna* (1966).

— the presence of the Whole in the fragment — by way of harmony or ordered numerical relationships. Yet it could render the no less pregnant idea of beauty as the Whole irrupting into the fragment and the fragment opening itself to be embraced in the depths of the unsayable Whole; and this by way of interruption, negation, surprise, silence, no less than of harmony, measure, and relationship, without excluding these latter a priori. Such a form of musical expression could turn out to be of help to the unquiet heart of this postmodern age. It could lead to the perception in the midst of this "shipwreck" of ancient certainties of a possible new way into a certainty which is neither ideological nor falsely consoling, but authentic and liberating. This is the certainty of knowing oneself welcomed into a higher, deeper safekeeping, where interruption and silence say no less than words, because here it is not the all-encompassing vision of the subject, nor the ordered equilibrium of the parts which transmits the divine, but precisely instead darkness, silence, all that which goes beyond what can be said and says even more.[43]

Besides the examples cited, to what extent can one say that such music exists today, speaking by its silence and silent in its speaking, revealing while concealing, and blossoming in its very incompleteness? It will fall to those who create and enjoy sacred music both now and in the future to answer this question; our hope, however, is that they may do this by holding together the courage of creativity — beyond any static repetition of or nostalgic return to the past, even while still responsibly appreciating the great tradition of sacred music — and docility to the Spirit and his unceasing, unpredictable surprises. . . .

However, it is and remains true that music — in all its forms and so in all the ways in which it becomes language — carries within it something perennially incomplete, a kind of tragic dimension, which is just as much the case, indeed perhaps even more so, for that music which aims at being the mediation of transcendence, as is the case with "religious" or "sacred" music:

> On the other hand, art is in itself tragic, since in it the Spirit which is immediate and ineffable wills to be realized in a form. But that is impossible. Music is the form which draws us closest to the Spirit, the finest veil which separates us from him. But it also shares the tragic destiny of all

---

43. Jankélévitch's *La musica e l'ineffabile* seems to move in this direction.

art, having to remain nostalgic and thus provisional. And precisely because it is closest to the Spirit, without ever being able to convey him fully, it is the most nostalgic of all.[44]

More than in any other art, in any music which seeks to be the language of the Transcendent one experiences how the wind of the Spirit "blows where it wills, and you can hear the sound it makes, but you do not know where it comes from or where it goes" (John 3:8). Perhaps because of this, sacred music more than any other evokes feelings of peace and nostalgia, of joy and melancholy: and perhaps, too, because of this, it remains and always will remain an incomplete language, a speech reaching beyond itself to the unsayable, a sound tending to evoke and rest in Silence, pressing incessantly beyond the frontiers — yet never entirely arriving. . . .

44. Balthasar, *Lo sviluppo dell'idea musicale,* p. 47.

Chapter Eight

BETWEEN ICON AND STORY

The Cinema and the Sacred

Is it possible to transmit faith through the cinema? Can a film mediate transcendence? And, more generally, can the cinematographer's art be a kind of *locus theologicus,* a document, that is, in which a thinking faith can identify reflections or traces of its object?[1] It is not the intention here to respond to these questions on the basis of an empirical analysis of what the cinema has in fact produced, but instead to sound out what might be the conditions for the cinema to be a mediation of transcendence, both in the sense of opening the viewer towards absolute Mystery, as well as potentially being a place where the transcendent and sovereign Other comes among us.

Once the problem is stated in these terms, it becomes clear that it is nothing other than one aspect of the more general question about theological discourse. How may we speak of Difference in the language of identity? How can we give expression to absolute Mystery in the historically conditioned and this-worldly terms of the means of communication available to us? Once we have clarified what the fundamental coordinates of human discourse about God in the light of his revelation are, it will also become possible to reach a deeper understanding of the languages of faith which most closely approximate those employed by the cinema (especially the icon and the story), and thus to indicate on what conditions the lan-

---

1. This chapter is a reworking of an address I gave to the World Symposium on Cinema and the Sacred held in the Vatican December 1-3, 1997, at the initiative of the Pontifical Council for Culture: the opportunity for an exchange with the experts and practitioners present on that occasion has undoubtedly helped me develop my ideas.

guage of the cinema can become a mediation — even if always analogical — of transcendence.

The Challenge of Theological Discourse

When believers speak of God they know they speak of the One concerning whom they should rather be silent. While aware of this paradox, they also know that they cannot but speak of him: by its very nature, the word of faith is a word about God (a λόγος concerning God, in the sense of the objective genitive), which by its very nature refers back to the word which God says about himself (τοῦ θεοῦ λόγος, "the word *of God*" in the sense of the subjective genitive). The word spoken by theology is thus as inevitable — inasmuch as it is an act of obedient response to what God says about himself in revelation — as it is pregnant with silence, hiatus, and expectation, given that it is historical and contingent like all human discourse. It speaks while being silent; it is silent while speaking; it listens by asking questions; it asks questions by listening. It is both a word that asks and a word that responds. Inasmuch as it is human discourse, the word of faith begins from the human person; and yet it is truly itself when it is willing to start from what the Other has said of himself: "Omnis recta cognitia Dei, ab oboedientia nascitur" (Calvin).

Between exodus, which is our condition as human beings in our unceasing search for and yearning after the greatest of Mysteries, and advent, in which the Word of God and his Silence have come to dwell in the time we ourselves inhabit, theological discourse is a word spoken at the frontiers: it stands at the border between exodus and advent, continually pointing first to the one and then to the other side, between the fragile earth on which our feet are planted and the unfathomable abyss where the Other dwells. Theological discourse is, as it were, crossed by two totally asymmetric paths: first, the way of the pilgrim, the searcher for meaning, yearning for a place to call home, there to find an anchor for the journey and the strength to fight the battle with death; and second — and without this the first would not even exist — the Origin, the beginning, premise, and foundation of all that is, comes to us from his unfathomable silence. At the linguistic level, analogy is the approach that holds these two distinct movements together in the abyss of the asymmetry that characterizes them. Analogy seeks to provide a foundation for the possibility of that proximity in infinite separateness and distance in proximity, which are postulated by the discourse of faith.

The doctrine of analogy is thus not born of abstract intellectual curiosity, but arises instead from the need to offer a considered justification for the theological use of human language. It is because faith speaks of God in obedience to revelation, and because the eternal Word pronounced himself in the words of time, that we experience the need to provide a foundation for affirmations made about the Mystery: the problem here is precisely how, when we speak of God, there can be continuity of meaning in the unbridgeable difference of that which is signified. Analogy draws together realities that are different, safeguarding their difference as well as demonstrating the proximity of the distances between them. This, of course, implies that the fixed point in analogical discourse about God is that God in the end cannot be spoken.[2] The via negativa has, however, dialectical value, and cannot be reduced to mere agnosticism. Nor is it possible to deny that something can in fact be positively said concerning God:[3] for believers the incontrovertible reason for this is the fact that there exist affirmations of faith founded on the words in which the Word who came among us pronounced himself.[4] Thus language, understood in this analogical sense, can be at the same time the place where the Other comes and the repetition of his exodus — revelation in the double sense of the self-offering here and now of what is veiled, and the renewed self-concealment of what is hidden. Precisely in the dialectical tension that characterizes analogy, it allows us to speak of the Absolute in words that are necessarily relative and in some fashion to express the Infinite and the Eternal in the inevitably deficient terms of space and time.

The Cinema: Where Icon Meets Story

So analogy is necessary if we are to speak of God, and it has been employed by theological discourse in a great variety of ways: of these, two especially

---

2. Cf. Aquinas, *In I Sent.* 34, 3, 2: "Convenientissimus modus signifcandi divina fit per negationem."

3. Cf. Aquinas, *Summa Theologiae* Ia, q. 13, a. 12: "Propositiones affirmativae possunt vere formari de Deo. . . ."

4. Cf. *Summa Theologiae, Sed contra:* "Propositiones quaedam affirmativae subduntur fidei, utpote quod Deus est trinus et unus, et quod est omnipotens."

can be identified in the language of the cinema, which results precisely
from bringing them together — the icon and the story.

The language of the *icon* can properly be understood in *symbolic* terms:
a "symbol" (σύμβολον) is that which holds together (σύν) without constric-
tion (βάλλεον, "to throw"). It is thus that which draws realities that are different from one another into relationship without, however, overlooking
their real difference, and it maintains the commonality of meaning between
them, even when one of the realities signified far surpasses or is discontinuous with the other. A symbol (like the related forms of parable and metaphor) "transposes": in it, analogy overcomes the incommunicability of
difference because the horizon of meaning employed is single and all-
encompassing, but it also avoids confusion because the realities signified
are not reduced the one to the other. Thus a symbol provides a unity of
meaning even when one of the realities signified far surpasses the other.

Further, it is precisely in the crisis that has befallen the totalitarian
claims of modern reason that the evocative power of the symbol is rediscovered: against a system of thought such as that found in the ideologies,
which claimed to be totally clear to themselves and to reduce the whole of
reality to this same kind of clarity, we have rediscovered the value of the
evocative, of that which draws together realities which are infinitely distant
the one from the other, yet without canceling those differences. In the
symbol, we are given to experience more meaning than can be articulated
or understood; new perspectives of thought and life are evoked; we sense
the touch of a new otherness, which provokes, nourishes, and discloses unexpected horizons; and we are invited to be open to a synthesis which ana-
lytic discourse cannot fully express. A system of thought which leaves
nothing in shadow and nothing unsaid is no longer admired as rich, but is
seen to be poorer than evocative and symbolic thought: the ideal does not
absorb the real, but must recognize that the real far surpasses it in power so
as to open itself and go beyond itself towards ever wider horizons.

It is precisely this dialectic between visible earthiness and invisible
depth that makes the icon so close to that mediation of transcendence
which is possible in the language of the symbol: "the icon is the vision of
things unseen."[5] An icon thus tends to communicate a twofold movement:

5. P. Evdokimov, *Woman and the Salvation of the World: A Christian Anthropology on the Charisms of Women,* trans. Anthony P. Gythiel (Crestwood, N.Y.: St. Vladimir's Seminary Press, 1994), p. 131. Cf. Chapter 6 above.

descent and ascent, distance approaching, closeness opening out on to distance. When read in faith, the icon is perceived as the place of divine Presence, where the Word of life appears among humankind, and humankind stands over that abyss of unfathomable Mystery whence the Word proceeds. In analogy with the mystery of the incarnate Son, the icon needs the bodiliness of color and the definiteness of form: what the Bible says with words, the icon proclaims with colors and makes present here and now.[6] To look at the "icon" thus means crossing the threshold towards Mystery, letting oneself be touched by the Transcendent in the forms of proximity.

It is thus in the context of revealed Mystery that the icon takes on all its symbolic meaning: glory hidden beneath the signs of history, the mystery at the same time implies the visibility of the events in which it is accomplished and the invisible depth of the divine work which is achieved in those events. The "icon" lives out of the same dialectic as Mystery, and only discloses its message to a reading that is open towards the abyss of the transcendent and sovereign Other. It is here that we can perceive a first theological possibility for the language of cinema: living as it does by a continuous succession of icons, this language can mediate transcendence in a manner analogous to the icon, with similar symbolic power, evoking that which is beyond in the forms of that which is close to us. The difference between the world of the icon and the cinema lies, however, in the fact that the succession of different scenes, which is constitutive of the latter, introduces a new element into the dynamic stillness of the icon. This decisive element is the story.

The *story* is indeed the other form in which analogical discourse makes its appearance in the language of the cinema. In coping with the logical limitations of identity imposed by dialectical mediation,

> the story works in a quiet and unpretentious way. It does not claim to possess the dialectic key, or to have received it from the hands of God — the key that would make it able to throw light on all the obscure processes of history without first having to pass through and overcome them. And yet all the same it does not travel in total darkness.[7]

Storytelling's analogical structure results especially from the "practical and performative sense of the narration": on the one hand, this tends "to the

---

6. Cf. Council of Constantinople IV (879): *DS* 654.

7. J. B. Metz, "Redenzione ed emancipazione," in *Redenzione ed emancipazione* (Brescia: Queriniana, 1975), p. 174.

practical communication of the experience it contains," and on the other, it makes it possible for "storyteller and audience to become part of the experience being narrated."[8] Obviously at work in the story is the same concern which underlies every form of knowledge, even the purely abstract and theoretical: the concern to evoke the experience, to make the narration a "linguistic action" in which word takes a hold on life.

One can understand how all this is important for every form of discourse that seeks to mediate transcendence: significantly,

> inasmuch as Christianity is the communion of those who have been redeemed in Jesus Christ, from its very beginnings it has not been primarily a communion of interpretation and discussion, but a communion bearing a memory and telling a story.[9]

Thus narrative theological language does not move in a foreign land; indeed, it finds a place in the narrative tradition that from very beginning has transmitted and actualized the gospel memory in time. It is, in any case, a matter of fact that very many groups and Christian movements "do not engage in discussion, but tell stories, or rather they try to tell stories. They tell their stories of conversion, they repeat the Bible stories." To reject this fact a priori would be a serious mistake: "Are we not stating something here which, in the public and official life of Christianity, seems to be too repressed?"[10]

And this is not to say that this practical and critical effect of storytelling is a kind of falling back into the sphere of the purely private or of matters of mere aesthetic preference:

> Do not there also perhaps exist, in our so-called post-narrative age, "storytellers" of the most varied kinds, who make us understand what stories can be [. . .] precisely not only artistic creations, private productions of whatever kind, but also stories which have an energizing effect upon society, stories which are in some measure socially critical and thus "dangerous"?[11]

8. Metz, "A Short Apology of Narrative," in *The Crisis of Religious Language: Concilium — Religion in the Seventies,* ed. J. B. Metz and J.-P. Jossa (London: Herder & Herder, 1973), p. 86.

9. Metz, "Redenzione ed emancipazione," p. 175.

10. Metz, "A Short Apology of Narrative," p. 88.

11. Metz, "A Short Apology of Narrative," p. 89.

In a post-ideological age like our own, one can go so far as to affirm that critical reason is never objective and disincarnate with respect to the living tradition in which it is placed, but that rather it needs memory and story-telling so as not to underestimate past suffering and succumb to the temptation of some form of abstract reconciliation. Only the many stories of passionate endeavor, recalled by narrative memory,

> break the spell of a total reconstruction of history by abstract reason and denounce the attempt to reconstruct awareness proceeding from the abstract unity of "I think." Such stories instead show how our awareness is an awareness "involved in stories" and which continues to identify itself in stories. After the dissolution of the idea of "historia magistra vitae," after the dethronement of the "magisterium" of history, this awareness of ours cannot give up the "magisterium of stories."[12]

Stories thus seem to guarantee critical reason's ability to take human history seriously; and it is stories that allow thought to mediate the contents of salvation history for present history in a reasoned fashion. Thus any theological discourse that in the name of the demands of science would sacrifice storytelling as pre-scientific would not only be falsely theological, but also falsely critical. In order to find a language which effects an authentic mediation of transcendence, the task which imposes itself is that of telling stories without giving up discursive thought, but placing the latter at the service of the narrative. And is not the language of the cinema of its very nature a way of telling stories that carry a reasoned argument, as it were, reasoning by way of stories? Here one can see how the narrative dimension — constitutive of the cinema — complements the icon's symbolic dimension: and it is by dint of this bringing together of icon and story that the cinema can be a language uniquely capable of mediating transcendence. But on what conditions?

Cinema and the Mediation of Transcendence

So, for cinema to be a language capable of mediating openness to Mystery and communicating Transcendence, the conditions for analogy must be

---

12. Metz, "A Short Apology of Narrative," p. 95.

respected: this means that we must give due attention to the twofold "no" and the decisive "yes" by which analogy lives. Thomas Aquinas's approach is important here, born as it is of the keen awareness of how in our attempt to speak of Mystery we always move between two possible extremes: clumsy attempts to make everything the same, such that the divine just becomes one more instance of what is already familiar and available, and extreme differentiation, which digs an unbridgeable trench of incommunicability between the world of God and the world inhabited by humankind. Aquinas's thinking on analogy is constructed between these two extremes:

> This way of holding things together stands in the middle between pure differentiation and mere sameness. Indeed, in the things said by analogy there is not one single reason, as happens in that which is the same; nor is there a reason which is totally different, as happens in that which is different; but the name which is thus said in such manifold ways indicates different proportions of one reality alone.[13]

Analogy draws together realities that are different, guarding them in their difference yet demonstrating the closeness of the differences.

The first "no" to be said in the use of any cinematographic language seeking to mediate transcendence is to extreme differentiation. A form of cinema which in its images or story excluded divine Mystery a priori or considered it in principle irrelevant and which thus simply became a photograph of a way of existing without transcendence, closed in upon itself and thus always returning to within the circle of the repetition of the subject and its projections, would not only not be a mediation of transcendence, but could also profoundly undermine the dignity of the human person, reducing this to the sphere of needs and appetites, of even the most violent and selfish kind. This is the case with the sadly abundant productions of pornographic cinema, but also with the kind of cinema which, in the name of *divertissement,* aims at anesthetizing people's awareness and extinguishing the true questions connected to the awareness of our own and others' pain. This kind of cinema often makes much money, but it is unproductive in terms of growth in the quality of life. Indeed, we can-

---

13. "Iste modus communitatis medius est inter puram aequivocationem et simplicem univocationem. Neque enim in his quae analogice dicuntur, est una ratio, sicut est in univocis; nec totaliter diversa, sicut in aequivocis; sed nomen quod sic multipliciter dicitur, significat diversas proportiones ad aliquid unum," *Summa Theologiae* Ia, q. 13, a. 5c.

not but consider that it contributes not a little to rendering human relationships ever more barbarous, and to that process of alienation which
promotes false models and creates false needs, inciting the viewer to
shorten the distance between desire and reality by way of imposition and
purely selfish and even violent appropriation.

The second "no" required here is to sameness of meaning: no matter
how much human discourse attempts to be a bearer of Transcendence, it
will never succeed in doing this in the strict sense — not even the cinema.
This is why any such presumption of sameness in the cinema issues both
in the genre of unbearably edifying films, where the shrill message of transcendence risks becoming artificial and an exercise in mere moralization,
as well as in ideological cinema, which — despite its claims to the contrary
— attempts to absorb the divine and the absolute in the excessively human
and relative horizons of preconceived theses. Whether the language of
sameness erases the human under the blinding light of the spiritualizing
message it is concerned to transmit, or whether it reduces the divine to the
horizon of an all-encompassing project inspired by an ideological understanding of humanity and history, it produces works which are mediocre
and entirely unsuitable to serve as mediations of transcendence. Further,
films produced along these lines shun all sense of aesthetic elevation, and
often lapse into banality and insipidity, with no evocative power or challenge to reflection. It is opportune here to recall Thomas Aquinas's appo-
site caution regarding representations of the divine, which are and always
remain this-worldly representations, and thus entirely unsuitable to render the simplicity of the divine essence:

> All that our understanding conceives of God does not succeed in repre-
> senting him, so that what is proper to the God always remains hidden
> from us, and the highest knowledge that we can have of him as we jour-
> ney through existence lies in recognizing that God is above everything
> that we can think of him,[14]

and — obviously — also above everything we can say of him in cinema's
combination of icon and story.

14. "Quidquid intellectus noster de Deo concipit, est deficiens a repraesentatione eius;
et ideo quid est ipsius Dei semper nobis occultum remanet; et haec est summa cognitio
quam de ipso in statu viae habere possumus, ut cognoscamus Deum esse supra omne id
quod cogitamus de eo," *De veritate* 2, 1, ad 9m.

So the "yes" we need here is to the *via media* characteristic of analogy, where proximity and distance do not follow an elliptical course away from one another, but rather hold to each other, albeit in the asymmetry of the relationship between them. This, too, is the decisive avenue for clarifying the conditions for the possibility of a cinema that can mediate transcendence. The closeness between different realities is founded on what is common to them both, that *unum commune* that can be understood in various ways and so provide the basis for various forms of analogy. If what unites realities which are distant from each other is thought of as the relationship of similarity between relationships, then the meeting point between the different realities which justifies the analogy is to be found in the similarity of the type of relationship to be found within the two couples of terms (the "analogy of proportionality" and the "analogy of attribution"). While the analogy of proportionality expresses less inadequately the incomparable distance between the ultimate and the penultimate, because it speaks of the relationship of relationships, the analogy of attribution, which concerns itself with levels of sharing in an *unicum,* underlines the continuity, in ever increasing distance, which subsists between the extremes. By bringing these two forms of analogy together, it becomes possible to safeguard the ever-increasing difference between the this-worldly and the divine of which we are speaking, while still in their albeit great proximity, as established by God's initiative, who turning toward the human person from the origins made us capable of that encounter of grace which is salvation.

It is precisely in this necessary interrelationship between these two forms of analogy that we can also understand the twofold presence and reciprocal roles of icon and story in the language of any cinema that seeks to mediate transcendence: one might say that the symbolic character of the icon is to the performative power of the story as the analogy of proportionality is to the analogy of attribution. Where the former expresses a similarity of relationships, in which the harmony in the fragment is the image of that in the Whole, the latter renders the idea of sharing, of continuity expressed in the succession of one story after another. Applying this rule to the language of the cinema, one could say that it must at the same time avoid saying too much and too little: saying too much would be tantamount to ignoring the abyss of distance indicated by the analogy of proportionality, but also presupposed by the graduality of attribution; saying too little would amount to neglecting the sharing in the *unum commune* supposed by the analogy of attribution, but also by the consistency of the relationships between relationships conceived within the horizon of pro-portionality. Saying too much would mean explaining away the symbol, giving up on the evocative power and living language of the metaphor, in favor of a flat and impoverishing reduction to the déjà vu, but also making of the story the exhibition of an argumentative thesis, instead of some-thing truly performative and open. Saying too little would amount to flat-tening the story into a mere recording of what is visible, without any performative and critical charge, but also emptying the symbol of its in-trinsic power to surpass and overtake.

So cinema capable of mediating transcendence will surprise by the ap-parent absence of explicit professions of faith: the form employed — at once symbolic and narrative — allows for an openness to Mystery, and for Mystery's appearance in the paradox of the opposite and unfinished. Yet this kind of cinema will also be convincing because it especially uses a nar-rative structure: thanks to story's performative power, this is capable of creating in the viewer an attitude of openness towards the Transcendent through the power of "dangerous," and thus critical and transforming, memories which are effectively "told." So we can say that the language of cinema — like every human discourse — can indeed express and make present transcendence, but on the condition that it maintains the tension proper to analogy. Cinema is especially predisposed to do this, though, more than any other form of communication, because it is peculiarly able to hold symbolic and narrative language together — the icon with its evo-cative power, and the story with its open-ended potential to involve the viewer. In the end, however, and as for every form of language, the decision about the message cinema offers, and the way it does this, lies in the minds and hearts of those who produce and enjoy it. . . .

Chapter Nine

MORTAL BEAUTY

At the Threshold

"Is not beauty the place where we must necessarily begin?" asks Cristina Campo. Faced with the way beauty has been so obviously forgotten, she quotes these lines from William Carlos Williams:

> But it is true, they fear
> it more than death, beauty is feared
> more than death, more than they fear death.[1]

Campo adds:

> And they are right, because to accept it is always to accept a death, an end of the old man and a difficult new life. . . . All people experience this terror, but most prefer to shoot beauty down or to take refuge in horror by forgetting it.[2]

There is something tragic about beauty: its kiss is deadly, precisely because the All that manifests itself in what is beautiful is ultimate, final, and extreme, and so underscores the frail nature of the fragment. And yet this very epiphany of Beauty in the "Infinite made tiny" can open up toward a singular victory over death. . . .

1. William Carlos Williams, *Paterson,* rev. ed., ed. Christopher MacGowan (New York: New Directions, 1992), p. 106.
2. C. Campo, *Sotto falso nome: A cura di M. Farnetti* (Milan: Adelphi, 1988), pp. 179-80.

Frail Beauty

When the All offers itself in the fragment it reveals the fragment's ineluctable finitude: what is beautiful makes plain the frailness of beauty. Beauty is like death, which "is impending for Dasein. Death is not something not yet present-at-hand . . . as such, death is something *distinctively*."[3] Like death, beauty comes unannounced and so is experienced as a threat: this is the fundamental reason why the experience of beauty is entwined with melancholy. Beauty reminds all those who dwell in time that here they have no lasting home, of how indeed this earth of theirs seems enveloped by the silence of nothingness. And since it is precisely in the confusion born of this sense of nothingness that anguish appears, it can readily be understood how full of anguish the experience of beauty may turn out to be: suspended over the abyss of death's silence, the human heart, drawn by beauty, becomes restless about its destiny.

> We don't know how we'll turn up
> tomorrow, hard-pressed or happy:
> perhaps our path
> will lead to virgin clearings
> where youth's water murmurs eternal;
> or maybe come down
> to the last valley in the dark,
> the memory of morning gone.
> Foreign lands
> may welcome us again; we'll lose
> the memory of the sun, the chime
> of rhymes will abandon the mind.
> Oh the fable that explains our life
> will suddenly become
> the murky tale that can't be told! . . .[4]

Here we can grasp why beauty unsettles us in a way we often seek to avoid: we flee from beauty as we flee from the thought of death. And this is

3. Martin Heidegger, *Being and Time*, trans. John Macquarrie and Edward Robinson (New York: Harper and Row, 1962), pp. 293-94.

4. Eugenio Montale, "Mediterranean," in *Eugenio Montale: Collected Poems, 1920-1954*, trans. Jonathan Galassi (New York: Farrar, Straus and Giroux, 1998), pp. 72-75.

indeed not only the experience of individuals, but also of humankind and of whole epochs: that optimistic spirit connected with adult and emancipated reason which dominated the modern era not infrequently relegated death to the condition of a mere moment of transition, simply an instant in that all-encompassing process of the Spirit which culminates in a victory assured from the outset. Death thus became a kind of "black flower," with no place in any human consciousness that had attained the bright day of self-possession:

> Consciousness first finds in self-consciousness — the notion of mind — its turning-point, where it leaves the parti-colored show of the sensuous immediate, passes from the dart void of the transcendent and remote super-sensuous, and steps into the spiritual daylight of the present.[5]

And Hegel adds:

> So that having got rid of the dark utterances of metaphysics, of the colorless communion of the spirit with itself, outer existence seemed to be transformed into the bright world of flowers — and there are no *black* flowers, as we know.[6]

The modern myth of progress, so dear to the "great narratives" of the ideologies, tends to turn death into just one, somewhat incidental, stage in the history of the individual totally taken up into the great cause, and so sacrificed to the triumph of the idea: in this scheme, death is ignored, avoided, concealed; death here becomes a fatuous "black flower" in the meadows of the Absolute. . . .

There is a connection, though, between this "decline of death" and a "decline of beauty": beauty is turned into a mere spectacle and reduced to a good for consumption, so that it can be deprived of its painful challenge and human beings helped not to think anymore, helped to flee the pain and passion of truth, to abandon themselves to whatever can be enjoyed here and now and whose value can be calculated exclusively in terms of immediate use. This is the victory of the mask over the truth; this is the nihilism that gives up the hope of being able to love, the attempt to flee from the pain

5. G. W. F. Hegel, *The Phenomenology of Mind*, trans. J. B. Baillie (London: George Allen & Unwin, 1931), p. 227.

6. *Hegel's Science of Logic*, trans. A. V. Miller (London: George Allen & Unwin, 1969), p. 26.

of nothingness, as we equip ourselves with calming masks behind which to hide from the tragedy of emptiness. In the great marketplace of the "global village" the signs of beauty seem to have disappeared; on all sides the mask of propaganda appears to triumph over the tragic seriousness of definitive truth and beauty. Thus we can see how the "eclipse of death" is inseparably bound to the "death of beauty": the fragile fragment seems no longer capable of bearing the weight of the All erupting in and through it. . . .

Beauty Beyond

And yet these times of ours, that follow on the end of what Eric Hobsbawm has called the "short century," are not entirely without signs of hope and of the search for true beauty. There is, in the words of Max Horkheimer, a widespread sense of a "longing for perfect and complete justice," which can also be recognized in the restless search for lost meaning. This is not "une recherche du sens perdu," a mere sense of the loss of things past, but rather the effort to rediscover beauty beyond the shipwreck, to make out an ultimate horizon against which to chart the journey traveled by all that is penultimate. Hans Blumenberg's metaphor of a "shipwreck with a spectator" brings out at one and the same time how all the actors in the present complex situation are children of modernity, both shipwrecked and spectators, and also how — precisely because of this — there is to be found in them both the disaster itself as well as the possibility of resisting it. Beyond the various forms of thought that seek to evade death and beauty, the question of meaning begins to reemerge, and with it the sense of how urgent it is to return to the mysterious beyond-ness of beauty that manifests itself in the fragility of existence: "restituer la mort," to use the phrase of Ghislain Lafont, is a task awaiting us all.

As we find the courage to set about such a task, we realize that the presence of the All in the fragment does not only make plain how fragile the fragment is, but also provides the horizon that guarantees the fragment's very dignity. Inasmuch as both death and beauty are the "verbum abbreviatum" of human finitude, they are at one and the same time lookouts for the absolute future, which is neither simply deducible from the present nor at its beck and call, as well as being in themselves the compendium of the whole enigma of the human condition. This is what is revealed to the eyes of faith by the death of the Son of God in the darkness of Good

Friday and by his rising to life, that fragment of time where the All broke into time in a definitive way. It is in the death and resurrection of the Humble One that Beauty most fully goes beyond herself, helping those who dwell in time to "go beyond" death and "redeem" the fragment.

When God goes out of himself and then returns to himself, Beauty comes and journeys towards final victory. The "exitus a Deo" of the Son who came in the flesh culminates in the event of his death, thus inseparable from absolute Mystery, the place of the supreme advent of the Eternal in the form of human finitude. The depth of the meaning of the death on the Cross is thus revealed by the other divine "going beyond," the "reditus ad Deum" of the Son made flesh, in which death was swallowed up by victory (cf. 1 Cor. 15:54). Between these two journeys outwards, which break the circle of a life imprisoned in the mortal silence of nothingness, the death of the Son of Man is to be seen as the event of the supreme abandonment and supreme communion of that Beauty which came in the flesh.

The supreme abandonment of crucified Beauty reveals in the crudest of ways the experience of the infinite fallenness of existence: "My God, my God, why have you forsaken me?" (Mark 15:34). This cry at the ninth hour witnesses to the condition of fragility of those who dwell in time, with which the Son made himself one: called to life from nothing, all living beings are bound around by nothingness, enveloped in the mysterious silence of the Beginning. No mysticism of death will be able to cancel death's dark side, the mysterious and dramatic aspect of this separation with no apparent return. The death of the Crucified One shows how dying, the supreme abandonment, leads to the threshold of the deepest separation from the Origin and thus to the most painful wound. We die alone: loneliness is and remains the inevitable price of the supreme hour:

> I am deeply grieved, even to death; remain here and stay awake with me. . . . Could you not stay awake with me one hour? . . . My God, my God, why have you forsaken me? (Matt. 26:38, 40; 27:46)

We die crying out as we did at our beginning, wounded then as now, proclaiming different kinds of birth: "We appear, we cry out: this is life; we cry out, we leave: that is death" (Ausone de Chancel). Beauty abandoned on the Cross reveals our deepest tragedy.

And yet the Crucified Christ also shows us the loving face of the hidden Other: "Father, into your hands I commend my spirit" (Luke 23:46).

The abandoned Son is in deep communion with the One who abandons him: he hands himself over, accepting the Father's will with loving obedience. The Father truly hands himself over, too: he does not spare his own Son (cf. Rom. 8:32). Jesus gives himself (cf. Gal. 2:20): he lives his death, the ultimate abandonment, as an act of freedom and of supreme acceptance. And so the Cross shows that it is possible to be at once very far, and very near: the pain of the furthest separation is transformed by the fire of love, which is as strong as death (cf. Song of Songs 8:6).

To die in the Beauty which dies is "to abandon oneself" into God's embrace, letting everything be transfigured in him who welcomes us into another, new Beauty. Beauty revealed on the cross reveals the littleness of the fragment, but also that it can be the place where we pass into the Mystery, thanks to the Son who came in the flesh once for all and made death his own. His death, the death of Beauty, opens the way for us to the impossible possibility of life, to the death of death, to the victory of ultimate Beauty over all that passes. . . .

At the Threshold . . .

Yet which of us can live like him, most beautiful of the sons of men, as in the hour of his death he draws communion and abandonment into one? Who like him can pass beyond the threshold? According to the faith of the New Testament distance and intimacy meet, thanks to the Consoler's power:

> Jesus said: "It is finished." Then he bowed his head and gave up the spirit. (John 19:30)

As the Spirit supports the abandoned Christ in the hour of his mortal destiny, the same Spirit keeps him united to God, making him able for the supreme sacrifice: this is the insight expressed in images of the "Trinitas in Cruce," wherein the death of the Crucified One is presented as the revelation of the Trinity. The Father bears in his arms the wood of the cross, from which hangs the Son enfolded in death, while the dove of the Spirit mysteriously separates and unites the abandoned Jesus and the One who abandoned him (see, for example, Masaccio's *Trinity* in the Church of Santa Maria Novella in Florence). Thus

Death has been swallowed up in victory. Where, O death, is your victory? Where, O death, is your sting? . . . Thanks be to God, who gives us the victory through our Lord Jesus Christ. (1 Cor. 15:54-55, 57)

Crucified Beauty leads us back to Beauty at the end victorious: beyond all the words spoken in history there is, and remains, the divine care, the hidden Beauty. At the end Beauty will be all in all, and the whole world will be his home, and then his silence, more eloquent than any word, will enfold all things: "Love never ends" (1 Cor. 13:8). Writes Karl Rahner:

Then you will be the last word, the only word that lasts, never to be forgotten. Then, when in death all things will fall silent, and I will have finished learning and suffering, there will begin that great silence, where you alone will speak, the Word from eternity to eternity. Then will cease all human speaking; to be and to know, to know and to experience, will have become the same thing. I will know as I am known, I will sense what you have said to me: yourself. No human word, no idea, will stand between you and me. You yourself will be the only word of jubilation, of love and of life, which fills every corner of my soul.[7]

To come before this ultimate beauty — the goal of Christian hope and promised vision — is the gift and challenge offered to the gaze of those who believe, provided they look to the One who has crossed the threshold once and for all: Christ, abandoned and risen, pledge and foretaste of glorious Beauty in his crucified flesh, offered for the Father and for us.

Grant me, Lord, that when lost
at the last I am going to depart
from this night of darkness in which the heart
dreaming is shriveled, I may enter into
the bright day that never ends, mine eyes fastened
on thy white body, Son of Man, complete
Humanity, in the light uncreated
that never dies; mine eyes fastened on thine,
oh Christ, and my gaze submerged in Thee, Lord![8]

7. K. Rahner, *Tu sei il silenzio,* 6th ed. (Brescia: Queriniana, 1988), pp. 34-35.

8. Miguel de Umamuno, *The Christ of Velazquez,* trans. Eleanor L. Turnbull, p. 132, © 1951, The Johns Hopkins University Press. Reprinted with permission of The Johns Hopkins University Press.

Neither, though, as we look on this crucified Beauty, foretaste of eternity, do we forget, or turn from, this world's fleeting beauty, to which our hearts are bound. Final Beauty is not only death, but also resurrection.

If the world's already so beautiful, Lord, if one sees it
with that peace of yours within this eye of ours,
what more can you give us in another life?

Therefore I'm jealous of this face, these eyes,
this body that you have given me, Lord, this heart,
that throbs here always . . . and fear so much to die!

With what other senses will you make me see
this blue sky-heaven that stands upon the mountains,
and the measureless sea, and the sun that shines on all things?
Give in these senses eternal peace, and I
will wish for no more heaven than this blue sky.

That man who to no moment would cry "Halt!"
(except the moment which might bring him death)
I don't understand him, Lord; I who would say
"halt" to so many moments of each day
to make them all eternal in my heart! . . .
Or is this "making eternal" already death?
But then, ongoing Life, what would that be?
No more than the shade of time that passes, falls,
the illusion of the far off and the near,
the count of the much and little, the cheap and dear,
deceiving count, since all that's already All.

Well, be it so! This world, whatever it be,
so various, so vast, so fugitive,
this land of earth, with all it makes to live,
is my native fatherland, Lord; and could it not be
also a native fatherland of heaven?
I am a man, and human is my measure
for all I could believe in or could hope:
if my faith and hope stop here and go no further,
will you count that a fault in me, beyond?

Beyond, I see sky-heaven and the stars,
and even up there I'd wish to be a man:
if you've made all objects to my eyes so fair,
if you've made my eyes, my senses for them here,
why shut them now, looking for another "like"?
If for me like this world no other shows!
That you are, Lord, I know; but where, who knows?
All that I look at, looks like you to me. . . .
Let me believe then, you are here to see.
And when that hour shall come, that hour of fear
in which these human eyes of mine close here,
open for me, Lord, greater ones, create
me eyes your boundless face to contemplate:
Let my death be a greater birth-time there![9]

The beauty of all that passes is the threshold that opens out on the horizons of the Beauty that does not pass. The Whole offers itself in the fragment; the fragment opens itself towards the Whole through *the door of Beauty*. . . .

9. The "Cant Espiritual" is among the most beautiful compositions of the Catalan poet Joan Maragall. The original, with a translation in Spanish, is published in his *Obra poética* (Madrid, 1984), vol. II, pp. 185-86. The English translation reprinted here is by David Lake and is available online at http://www.stihi.ru/poems/2004/05/29-698.html, accessed July 2008.